WHERE THE HEART IS

John Boorman is the internationally distinguished film director. His most recent film, *Hope and Glory*, depicted his childhood experiences in Britain during the Second World War.

Telsche Boorman went to Paris to study at the Sorbonne, and has remained there ever since, where she has written film scripts as well as participating in the School-Aid project to bring famine relief to Ethiopia. She is married to the editor of the French edition of *Rolling Stone* and has a daughter, Daphne.

WHERE THE HEART IS
Telsche Boorman and
John Boorman

faber and faber

LONDON · BOSTON

First published in 1990
by Faber and Faber Limited
3 Queen Square London WC1N 3AU

Photoset by Parker Typesetting Service Leicester
Printed in Great Britain by Richard Clay Ltd Bungay Suffolk

A CIP record of this book is available from the British Library

ISBN 0–571–14328–8

CONTENTS

John Boorman lining up the shot with Susy Amis (CHLOE).

INTRODUCTION

Telsche, my eldest daughter, and I were cruising down the Nile in December 1987. We planned to develop an idea for a film between excursions to the temples and tombs. She also wanted to get pregnant. She circled a fertility stone in Luxor the requisite seven times and later found that she was. We completed the screenplay during her gestation, or we thought we had. As it turned out, we were still rewriting when her daughter, Daphne, was three months old, and again when she was six months – twelve drafts in all. And it turned out in a way we could never have imagined when we were sailing through the dreamscapes of Egypt.

Hope and Glory opened in September 1987 in London and a couple of months later in America. It was surprising that a piece as private and particular as this should connect to people across the world, but what pleased me more was simply making them laugh. It prompted Telsche and me to contemplate a contemporary family comedy, drawing on our own experiences and observations rather as I had done in *Hope and Glory*. I had been nursing the idea of a modern Lear, master of a business empire who walks out, dividing it among his offspring. I had Sean Connery in mind and he and I chewed it over from time to time. Actors of a certain age begin to meditate on Lear. And not only actors. The mad king was often in my thoughts.

Telsche's idea was more a state of being, a condition rather than a story. She was interested in how her sisters and brother and their friends were in a permanent state of preparation, getting ready, living in a tumescence of anticipation. She wanted to explore that.

We put these strands together and began to pillage the family history and scavenge the lives of friends. My daughter Katrine had recently married into the Conran family. When the two eldest sons, Sebastian and Jasper, went to art college, their father, Sir Terence, rather than make them an allowance, gave them instead the use of a house he owned. They would have to earn their money from letting out rooms and thus rub up against market forces. In our story, the father, Stewart McBain, head of a demolition company, finds himself stuck with a house he cannot knock down. He drives out his three grown children from the family home and obliges them to make their own lives in this house. Some of Sebastian's and Jasper's tales of the mess they made of this arrangement found their way into our story. Sir Terence has been hounded by corporate raiders so in the film we applied that pressure to Stewart; Stewart's diatribe on page 32 is paraphrased from him.

The character of Chloe, the artist, is drawn from Timna Woollard, a childhood friend of Telsche and Katrine. Timna developed a technique of painting bodies into landscapes and photographing them. It is Timna herself who does the striking paintings in the film which are attributed to Chloe.

Daphne is based on my third daughter, Daisy, twin of Charley, who is, in turn, the inspiration for Jimmy, the third of the three McBain children.

We aimed to make a diversion, an entertainment that turned on certain social observations, but dark issues, serious matters, inevitably intruded. Our comedy held them at bay, but they hovered on the edge of things. The shadow cast by this sunny comedy is this: the fear of all of us who enjoy material comforts – possessions, houses, cars, chattels – the fear that this well-being might some day be snatched from us.

Lear gives up power, authority, position, becomes the lowest of creatures, spurned, mad. Stewart is ruined by the system, plumbs the depths, tastes despair and madness.

Now that the Third World is no longer a geographical concept, oceans away, now that it is all about us in New York, in London, the cold fingers of that fear creep up on us. I look into the faces of the street people and I see men like myself. As I shamefully spurn their pleas or guiltily shower them with money, I recognize my own frailty in their eyes. And walking home I reflect that we might all be homeless soon, in the most terminal way, if the planet can no longer endure our demands and excesses.

I go back to the bosom of my family, a group of ecologically conscious reconstructed consumers, yet still consuming more than our just share. We are caring and supportive of each other, we are well stocked with fine wines and gourmet organic food, the greatest writers fill my shelves and the world's music mutely awaits my whim. Good land and mature trees separate us from the inconvenience of neighbours. We are bored by politics, tolerant, fairly free of prejudice, lacking in both conviction and passionate intensity. Or so it seems. We are conscious of our luck. Into our house television spills the miseries of the world beyond. We sorrow dutifully, yet often the truer emotion is a squirming embarrassment at our good fortune.

Telsche's contention is that in these cocoons of privilege the young are preparing, are getting ready for they know not what. Is it a rehearsal for another life, or at least a new dawning? They are vamping till ready. We agreed that my offspring and the middle-class progeny of those about us, in their late teens and twenties, lack the ambition of their parents. They are imaginative and inventive but are not driven. They smile and shrug when confronted with a world in turmoil. They turn in on themselves, dreaming, re-inventing the world through the imagination.

We wrote the early draft partly in Paris, partly in Ireland, between Christmas and spring 1988, our concentration broken only by Telsche's occasional nausea and my dashing off to America or London to pick up awards for *Hope and Glory*. Our story was set in London, but I failed to raise the finance to make it as a British film. We transposed it to New York, which turned out to be so expensive that we were obliged to shoot the interiors in Toronto. Fourteen months after our journey on the Nile I found myself in the winter wastes of Canada building sets in a dusty warehouse. The film was shot from mid-April until the end of June 1989 and edited here in Ireland.

John Boorman, Annamoe, Ireland

CAST

STEWART	Dabney Coleman
JEAN	Joanna Cassidy
CHLOE	Susy Amis
DAPHNE	Uma Thurman
JIMMY	David Hewlett
THE SHIT	Christopher Plummer
LIONEL	Crispin Glover
TOM	Dylan Walsh
OLIVIA	Emma Woollard
HARRY	Maury Chaykin
HAMILTON	Ken Pogue
JOHN	Michael Kirby

Producer/Director	John Boorman
Script	Telsche Boorman and John Boorman
Associate Producer	Sean Ryerson
Executive Producer	Edgar Gross
First Assistant Director	Tony Lucibello
Director of Photography	Peter Shuschitsky
Art Director	Carol Spier
Body Paintings	Timna Woollard
Set Decorator	Eleanor Galbraith
Costume Designer	Linda Matheson
Sound	Brian Day
Editor	Ian Crafford
Music	Peter Martin
Continuity	Susan Haller
Photographer	Atilla Doret

EXT. DEMOLITION SITE. DAY
Main titles over.
A building collapses in Brooklyn. STEWART MCBAIN, *his*
FOREMAN *and a policeman are at a table with detonating equipment.*
STEWART *is entranced by the perfection of his destruction. He*
prepares the detonator for the collapse of a second building. He pushes
the fire button, 'conducting' the destruction that follows.

A wall collapses, revealing a lone house with a crumbling but romantic
Dutch façade which stands in the middle of the demolition site.

HARRY, *Stewart's lawyer, runs up to him.*
HARRY: Stewart! I just got off the phone with Jack. He told me
    there's a possibility of some picketers . . . picketing.
STEWART: Did he?
    (STEWART *sees that the house is indeed surrounded by picketers,*
    defying the advancing bulldozers. Their placards say: 'Support
    Landmark Status for the Dutch House'.)

EXT. DEMOLITION SITE. DAY
The site is practically cleared. Only the Dutch House remains. An
official staples a preservation order on the front door of the house. The

I

picketers celebrate. A limousine and a TV van pull up. STEWART *leaps out of the limo, followed by* HARRY. *They are pursued by a TV reporter.*

HARRY: It's completely absurd. A monstrosity like that, by a
  third-rate architect. How was I to know the *New York Times*
  would declare him a genius?

STEWART: (*Shaking his head*) They're turning this town into a
  tomb, Harry, making every rat-infested ruin a monument.
  (*Yelling at the picketers*) Yeah, save the city for the
  cockroaches!

HARRY: (*Yelling at the picketers*) Please go away!
  (*To* STEWART) Is there any way to build around it?
  (STEWART *points to the hoarding which depicts the post-modern
  high-rise block he proposes to build on this site.*)

STEWART: Yeah. The tallest tower in Brooklyn with a little pimple
  on its bottom. Good thinking.
  (STEWART *reaches the cheering picketers. He glares at them.
  Suddenly he recognizes his daughter* DAPHNE, *who has just
  pushed her way to the front of the group. He turns to* HARRY,
  indignantly) Oh my God, that's my daughter.
  (*To* DAPHNE) Daphne . . . Honey . . . You know, I
  understood when you stuck up for the whales and the
  rainforests, but to betray your own father for a broken-down
  Dutch toilet . . .

DAPHNE: (*Shouting back*) I'm not with them. Mom sent me down here to tell you not to be late tonight.

STEWART: (*Disconcerted*) Well, it's just the kind of thing you would do.

DAPHNE: (*Furious*) Right . . .

(DAPHNE *grabs the nearest placard, holds it up and shakes it at her father. The picketers join in with* DAPHNE, *shouting for the TV cameras.*)

INT. STEWART'S BROWNSTONE HOUSE. HALLWAY. EVENING
As STEWART *comes through the front door, he is met with a blast of rock music. It hits him like a blow between the eyes. He looks like a man about to unravel, trying hard to hang on. He peels off his dripping raincoat and is jabbed in the kidneys by the handlebars of his son Jimmy's ten-speed gleaming bike, which is parked awkwardly in the hall. His other daughter,* CHLOE, *comes clattering down the stairs clutching cans of film, assisted by the housekeeper,* MRS JOSE.

CHLOE: (*Distraught*) Please, let me take the limo, Dad, I'll send it right back for you.

STEWART: (*Rubbing his side*) Out of the question.

CHLOE: It's raining, I'm crazed. You want to ruin the most important night of my life?

3

STEWART: It's my fault you're late? I made it rain?

MRS JOSE: Mr McBain, you should be ashamed. Your little girl.

CHLOE: (*Kissing him*) Thanks, Dad. Saw you on TV. Sorry.

(The driver, JOSE, comes through the front door carrying Stewart's briefcase.)

C'mon, Jose. We're on our way.

(JOSE thrusts the damp briefcase into STEWART's arms with an apologetic shrug and takes Chloe's things. STEWART climbs the stairs. As CHLOE leaves, she calls out to JIMMY to hurry up. JIMMY strides out from the kitchen, carrying a 16-mm projector. He bumps the wall with it. STEWART spins round, pointing an accusing finger at the bicycle.)

STEWART: Jimmy, the bike.

JIMMY: Sorry, Dad. That acid rain murders the chrome.

(He edges his way towards the door. He turns back, smiling, teasing.)

Saw you on TV, Dad. 'A victor*ee* for the Committ*ee* to save the cit*ee*!'

(STEWART glares at him, which wipes the smile off Jimmy's face. JIMMY slinks out. The rock music hits a particularly loud passage. STEWART winces. He turns back down the stairs into the living-room.)

INT. LIVING-ROOM. NIGHT

STEWART *enters. The effect of the eighteenth-century antiques and the Baccarat chandeliers is marred by a pile of electronic hi-fi and computer equipment connected by a tangle of cables.* STEWART *throws switches and hits buttons, but the music blares on. He reaches over and rips out the electric plug from the wall.*

INT. STAIRS AND LANDING. NIGHT

STEWART *climbs the stairs again. Shoes and tights are scattered on the stairs.* DAPHNE *looks over the rail of the floor above, on which more clothes are draped.*

DAPHNE: Who stopped the music?

STEWART: I did. *Me.* Your dad. The laughing stock of New York. I stopped it. For ever.

(JEAN, his wife, half-dressed, peers down.)

JEAN: (*Pleased*) You're late.

STEWART: Are you ready?

4

JEAN: No, not quite.
STEWART: So how can *I* be late?

INT. DESIGN SCHOOL. NIGHT
Girl students model wild clothes, moving to the pounding beat of rock music. They parade down a 'runway', jutting from a stage, on which is inscribed: 'Students' Graduation Show'.

EXT. DESIGN SCHOOL. NIGHT
STEWART *guides his wife* JEAN *and daughter* DAPHNE *through the teeming rain and into the design school.* JEAN *has a Bloomingdales' plastic bag over her head to protect her hair. Daphne's bag is from Jasper Conran. Since they cannot see,* STEWART *holds their elbows and steers them. They bump into the door before he can open it. They turn their heads towards him in blind accusation. He is very wet.*

INT. DESIGN SCHOOL. NIGHT
A young flamboyant student, LIONEL, *who has designed the clothes, leads the models out into the outrageous finale. The audience of thrilled parents and friends applauds ecstatically. A panel of teachers, famous designers and artists makes notes and tries to maintain a judicious neutrality.*

LIONEL *catches the eye of his father, who beams up at him proudly. His father,* JOHN, *sees* STEWART, JEAN *and* DAPHNE *shaking off rainwater from their coats as they enter. He waves at them, indicating the empty seats beside him.* STEWART *gives a last shake of his body, like a sheepdog, spraying several people. The walls are hung with student paintings and fashion illustrations. Pottery and sculpture are on display.*

CHLOE, *their other daughter, wrapped in a cloak, comes up to them.*
CHLOE: I'm up next.
      (She guides them to their seats.)
JEAN: Don't worry about the limo, Chloe, we managed to find a
      cab.
      *(*STEWART *takes Jean's arm and leads her to the seats.* DAPHNE
      follows. CHLOE *runs to the stage.)*

INT. DESIGN SCHOOL. NIGHT
CHLOE *stands before a lowered screen.*

5

CHLOE: For my degree work I have made a film. For it I have
    developed a technique based on eighteenth-century *trompe*
    l'œil. It involves painting on the human body. In this case
    my own and my sister Daphne's, whom I would like to
    thank.
    (*DAPHNE smiles, flattered and proud. Her mother squeezes her*
    arm. CHLOE *signals up to a projector which has been situated at*
    the front of the balcony.)

INT. BALCONY. NIGHT
A young man, TOM, *is standing by the projector. He has been*
watching anxiously for her signal.
TOM: Go!
    (*In his excitement* TOM *brings down his fist, hitting his friend*
    JIMMY *painfully on the top of the head.* JIMMY *winces but*
    manages to get the projector going. JIMMY *gives* TOM *a*
    retaliatory punch, but Tom's eyes are fixed on CHLOE. JIMMY
    clutches his head in delayed reaction to the pain.)

IMAGES ON SCREEN
Painted, naked bodies merge into and emerge from backgrounds of
bizarre landscapes. A moving trompe l'œil.

CHLOE *appears on the screen, her naked body painted.*

CHLOE: 'The body is an infinite landscape painted by the soul',
Baudelaire.

INT. DESIGN SCHOOL. NIGHT
STEWART *looks at his wife as though what he is seeing is her fault.*
JEAN: (*Defensively*) It's art, darling, you just look at it. You don't
    have to understand it.
    (*Despite defending it,* JEAN *does not look totally convinced*
    herself.)

IMAGES ON SCREEN
A painted face against a seascape. The face moves, revealing that it is
painted on to DAPHNE's *torso. She opens her eyes, stares defiantly at*
the audience and winks.

INT. DESIGN SCHOOL. NIGHT
STEWART *lets out a strangled cry. He turns his pained face to*
DAPHNE. *She meets his eye boldly, then winks like she did in the film.*

IMAGES ON SCREEN
Chloe's body is a Picasso cubist painting.

INT. PROJECTION BOOTH. NIGHT
Tom's eyes widen.
TOM: Your sister's even more . . . you know . . . than I imagined.

IMAGES ON SCREEN
*The film concludes with Chloe's painted face. She signs off with the
title of her film:*

CHLOE
'People, Paint, Illusions', Chloe McBain

INT. LATER. DESIGN SCHOOL. NIGHT
The audience is standing around, sipping wine. STEWART *is talking to
Lionel's father,* JOHN.
STEWART: Education, I believed in it, I paid plenty for it and all

she's got to show for it is a pornographic film.

JOHN: At least she's . . . normal.

STEWART: You call that normal?

(JOHN *looks across at* LIONEL, *the dress designer, who is being congratulated by admirers.*)

JOHN: Well, she's not a . . . you know . . . like my boy Lionel.

STEWART: You put him through college, now put him out on his own. That'll shape him up.

JOHN: He's got it too good at home. (*He embraces the assembly with a sweep of his arm.*) I'd wager half these parents are victims of the 'won't-leave-home' syndrome. How do you get them out of the house?

STEWART: How? (*An idea strikes him with the force of a revelation.*) You do it with cunning and surprise and you harden your heart. At their age I already had my first ball and chain. (*JEAN appears at his side.*)

JEAN: Is he boring you with his balls and chains?

(CHLOE, JIMMY *and* DAPHNE *are standing by the stage. Friends pass and kiss* CHLOE, *congratulating her.*)

DAPHNE: Was I pretty in it?

JIMMY: Daphne, all we saw was your tits, and we couldn't see them for paint.

DAPHNE: But objectively, do you think the parts you saw were pretty?

JIMMY: No one could possibly recognize you.

DAPHNE: (*With a pained expression*) Dad recognized me.

CHLOE: (*Devastated*) He hated it. They all hated it!

JIMMY: Not all of them. Some of them were just bored. No. No. No. Only kidding.

DAPHNE *and* JIMMY: They loved it.

(DAPHNE *and* JIMMY *hug and squeeze their sister.* LIONEL *comes running up and flings his arms around the three of them. They all congratulate each other.*)

LIONEL: This truly amazing man has just offered me a contract to produce my own collection. Can you believe it?

JIMMY: So how much is he paying you?

LIONEL: (*Annoyed*) It doesn't work like that, Jimmy! They're giving me a huge cut of the profits.

(*Their friend* TOM *swaggers up to* CHLOE. *From behind his back he produces a bunch of tiger lilies that he presses into her arms.*

8

CHLOE *stiffens.*)

TOM: (*Suavely*) Chloe, that was amazing . . . What can I say? Roll over Picasso.

(CHLOE *cringes behind the flowers.* DAPHNE *smiles adoringly at* TOM.)

JIMMY: Picasso? You never looked at a painting before you met Chloe.

TOM: Chloe's work has opened my eyes.

JIMMY: Flies.

(*Lionel's father,* JOHN, *comes over to them. He turns to* CHLOE.)

JOHN: Aesthetically provocative and stunningly sexy. How would you like to create a calendar for a client of ours, an insurance company?

CHLOE: You mean for money?

JOHN: Quite a substantial amount.

CHLOE: It's very flattering, but I want to be a serious artist.

JOHN:(*Prickly*) The most serious artists in New York work in advertising. I'd venture to say that it's the only true art of our times. Think about it, Chloe.

(JEAN *throws her arms around* CHLOE.)

JEAN: I'm so proud of you, Chloe.

INT. LIMOUSINE. NIGHT

JEAN *sits between her two daughters,* CHLOE *and* DAPHNE, *on the back seat. She is hardly visible as their voluminous dresses billow over her.* STEWART *and* JIMMY *face them on the jump seats.*

JEAN: (*Solemnly*) Girls, you have the world at your feet. Try not to trip over it.

(CHLOE *and* DAPHNE *exchange a perplexed glance.* JIMMY *looks out the window.*)

JIMMY: Dad, we're crossing the Brooklyn Bridge!

(CHLOE *and* DAPHNE *feign shock-horror.*)

DAPHNE: Crossing the river?

CHLOE: Leaving Manhattan?

(JIMMY *taps on the glass partition.*)

JIMMY: Hey, Jose, wrong way.

STEWART: No. I'm putting you on the right way. The straight and narrow.

(*The limo turns off the bridge and down to the demolition site, where the Dutch House now stands alone. It is surrounded by*

9

mud and rubble. STEWART *indicates the house.*)
STEWART: Do you love it? Ugly is 'in' this year. Everybody just
    loves it.

EXT. DUTCH HOUSE. NIGHT
They climb out of the car and view the house without enthusiasm.
STEWART *starts towards it.*
CHLOE: It's poetic, like a flower stopping a tank.
STEWART: I'm giving it to you kids. Good. You like it.
CHLOE: What!
    (JEAN *studies their reactions nervously.*)
JEAN: (*Doubtfully*) I guess I could fix it up. With the right designer.
DAPHNE: Oh, I don't think we're ready to live on our own, Dad.
STEWART: Think of it as a survival test.
JIMMY: (*Brightening*) You mean it's only a game?
    (STEWART *unlocks the front door and slaps the keys into Jimmy's
    hand.*)
STEWART: It's a game. Exactly. And with very strict rules. No
    designers. You fix it up yourselves. You'll each get, let's say,
    seven hundred and fifty dollars. And the game starts right
    now.

(STEWART *throws a bunch of keys into Jimmy's unwelcoming hands.*)

DAPHNE: Right now?

CHLOE: But what do we do when we've used up the seven-fifty?

(STEWART *turns back to the car. They find his air of resolution scary.*)

STEWART: Use your wits. Find ways of making money.

DAPHNE: I suppose getting a job would be cheating?

STEWART: No. Jobs are good. Jobs are allowed.

JIMMY: It doesn't sound like a game. It sounds like real life.

(STEWART *starts back to the car, followed by* JEAN *and* DAPHNE.)

STEWART: What an adventure! Your own place. Do what you like. Play that music as loud as you like.

DAPHNE: (*To* JEAN) You can't spoil us and then stop spoiling us when it suits you.

(STEWART *holds the car door open for* JEAN.)

STEWART: Get in, Jean.

JEAN: You're being unreasonable, Stewart. They can't move in right away. The house is a ruin.

STEWART: Get in the car, Jean.

JEAN: I will not abandon my children.

STEWART: Get in the car, Jean. Home, Jose!

(JEAN *reluctantly gets into the limo, followed by* STEWART. DAPHNE *suddenly appears at the window of the car.*)

DAPHNE: I have no interest in playing this game!

STEWART: There'll come a day when you'll thank me for this.

(*The limo drives off.* DAPHNE *runs after the car, pounding on it.*)

DAPHNE: I will not . . . C'mon, Jose. I covered for you . . . C'mon, Mom . . . Who's gonna curl your hair?

(DAPHNE *finally gives up as the limo speeds away. She walks back to* JIMMY *and* CHLOE, *who have been watching incredulously. They look at each other and forlornly turn towards the Dutch House and start walking up to it.*)

EXT. DEMOLITION SITE. DAY

STEWART, HARRY *and* HAMILTON, *Stewart's banker, are walking the site, moving towards the Dutch House.* STEWART *strides ahead of the other two.*

HARRY: (*To* HAMILTON) Stewart has made demolition an art.
　　You've got to trust this guy. Give him a little time. Believe me,
　　he's a lot more stable than most people give him credit for.
STEWART: Hamilton, my company has destroyed more buildings
　　than World War Two. I have the capacity to flatten
　　Manhattan.
HAMILTON: Stewart, your expertise is not at issue here, but if you
　　can't develop this site, you're stuck with an enormous loan,
　　and the meter's running on the interest.
STEWART: You mean your bank's stuck with me.
　　(*They have arrived at the Dutch House.* STEWART *pauses for a
　　moment, looking at the house.*)
　　The way I feel, I'd like to tear down the place with my bare
　　hands.
　　(*He starts to attack the house;* HARRY *struggles to restrain him,
　　clutching him by the throat.*)
HARRY: Why don't we bulldoze it? Pay the fine. Take the heat.
　　Let's do it.
STEWART: (*Choking*) Yeah. And then what?
　　(HARRY *releases him and* STEWART *turns away.*)

HARRY: (*Looking across at* HAMILTON, *deflated*) They'd withdraw
    our building permits for the tower.
    (HAMILTON *looks extremely uncomfortable. He peers in through
    the conservatory windows.*)
HAMILTON: I believe you've got squatters.

INT. LIVING-ROOM/CONSERVATORY. DAY
The three siblings are recovering from their first night in the house.
CHLOE *comes out of the kitchen drinking water from a jar.* JIMMY *is
getting up from a makeshift bed.* DAPHNE *has been trying to warm
herself with some old newspapers, which she then starts to read. She
glances up and sees her father and two men peering in.*
DAPHNE: Chloe, there are three dirty old men peering in at us.
    And one of them is our father.
CHLOE: Make out like we're having a great time. It'll drive him
    crazy.
    (CHLOE *and* DAPHNE *start to dance.* JIMMY *seems at first
    nonplussed, but then starts to jump around like an ape, beating
    his chest.*)
DAPHNE: (*While dancing, with a happy expression on her face*) This

is child abuse. I'll report him to the Bureau of Child Welfare.
I hope Mother leaves him.

CHLOE: And then he'll end up a lonely old man.

DAPHNE: And serve him right.

EXT. DUTCH HOUSE. DAY

STEWART: Would you believe that boy dropped out of Harvard
and not out of a tree.

(STEWART *hangs his head.* HARRY *helps him away.*
HAMILTON *follows.* JEAN *arrives behind them with a trailer
bearing the children's possessions.*)

INT. LIVING-ROOM. DAY

CHLOE: He's gone. Did you see the look on his face?

DAPHNE: I'll do something awful and he'll never forgive himself.

JIMMY: He'll make us sweat it out here for a couple of days, then
we'll be back at the house, same as ever.

CHLOE: But a little more humble.

DAPHNE: I will never eat humble pie.

(*Suddenly they see* JEAN *at the window, beckoning to them.*)
It's Mother. She's come for us. We're going home.

JIMMY: They kick us out and they're still swarming all over us.

(*They all race to the window. Behind* JEAN *they see the open
trailer piled high with their belongings, including Jimmy's
bicycle.* JEAN *shrugs apologetically. They look at each other,
stunned.*)

CHLOE: He really means it this time.

JIMMY: I think we've been outmanoeuvred here.

DAPHNE: If only I could put my life in rewind and go back to the
womb.

EXT. DUTCH HOUSE. DAY

JEAN *is helping* CHLOE *and* DAPHNE *unload the trailer.* JIMMY
heaves a mattress on to his back and starts towards the house.

JEAN: I wept when I saw your empty rooms at home.

JIMMY: We wept when we saw the empty rooms here. (*He
staggers into the house.*)

(DAPHNE *starts to pull out different objects, grouping them
together on the rubble. She lifts out a computer screen and
keyboard and places them on to a different pile near by. This pile*

is obviously Jimmy's. There are other bits and pieces of electronics and computers, a trainset and a cardboard box full of Matchbox cars. There are beds, a few armchairs, a table and chairs.)

JEAN: You always said you couldn't wait to leave home.

CHLOE: You didn't believe us, did you?

DAPHNE: That was just to scare you.

(CHLOE *throws a suitcase on Daphne's pile.)*

That's my pile, Chloe. You organize your own pile.

CHLOE: All right, Daphne, all right. It's only a pile.

DAPHNE: Maybe, but it's the only pile I have. That pile is my past.

(CHLOE *pulls some more of her things from the back of the trailer. Paintbrushes, paints, canvases, finished paintings.* DAPHNE *takes out a child's chair and sits on it, overcome with nostalgia for her childhood.* JIMMY *returns to the trailer and takes his computer lovingly into his arms and heads back to the house.* JEAN *watches him with a sad smile.)*

JEAN: At least you'll have your toys, Jimmy.

(JIMMY *turns, clutching the computer.)*

JIMMY: This is not a toy, Mom. This is my future. This is the future of the world.

(JEAN *lifts a large painting down from the trailer. It is a copy of Manet's* Déjeuner sur l'Herbe. *Her head peeks over the top.)*

JEAN: Remember, Chloe? You copied it during your semester in Paris.

(CHLOE *takes the painting.* JEAN *follows her back towards the house, taking three envelopes from her purse.)*

Here's the money your father promised.

(*She gives the kids the money.* DAPHNE *takes hers reluctantly.)*

DAPHNE: You'll lend us more if we're really broke, won't you, Mom?

JEAN: No, I won't.

DAPHNE *and* CHLOE: (*Shocked)* Won't?

JEAN: That would be disloyal to your father. I know things have changed now, but I promised to love, honour *and* obey.

JIMMY: Our parents!

CHLOE: Remember how embarrassed we were in school? The only kids whose parents weren't divorced.

DAPHNE: And it was even worse when they found out our dad was in the House Wreckers' Union.

15

(*They all laugh, verging on the hysterical.* JEAN *looks at them fondly.*)

JEAN: You'll manage. More than manage. You'll make this house into something wonderful. Rent out rooms. Be independent and proud and true to yourselves.
(*She's moved by her words, but the children look at each other perplexed. Are both parents going out of their minds?*)

EXT. DUTCH HOUSE. DAY
The Dutch House sits forlornly amongst the rubble. There are puddles of water across the mud. Stepping-stones reach up to the front door. A Wall Street type looks at the sign announcing 'Rooms To Rent'. He looks furtively about him and starts towards the house.

INT. DUTCH HOUSE LIVING-ROOM. DAY
CHLOE *and* JIMMY *are painting the walls with rollers, moving them back and forth in time to the music playing on the stereo.* DAPHNE *is on her knees, scrubbing the floor. She is crying.*

CHLOE: Don't be such a baby.

DAPHNE: I'm not crying for myself. I'm crying for the people who had to do this for us all our lives. Mary and Mrs Jose. Even Mom once or twice.
(JIMMY's *face lights up as he sees the prospective lodger picking his way across the stepping-stones.*)

JIMMY: Hey! We've got a live one!
(JIMMY *and the girls run over to the window and look out expectantly. The Wall Street type pauses on each stone, hugging his briefcase to his chest as he jumps to the next stone. He takes a large step and, straddled between two stones, he slides pitifully into the mud. The three hopeful faces collapse in disappointment.*)

INT. CELLAR STEPS AND BOILER ROOM. DAY
JIMMY *strides down the steps into the boiler room. He starts to attack an antiquated boiler. He kicks it and beats it with a crowbar, grunting like a frenzied Samurai.*

INT. LIVING-ROOM. DAY
The steam pipes ring and splutter from Jimmy's blows. DAPHNE *is huddled over her schoolbooks.* CHLOE *is breaking up a chair and*

16

feeding it on to the feeble fire that is burning in the grate. DAPHNE
sweeps her books violently on to the floor.

DAPHNE: (*Dressed in coat and gloves*) I was so happy studying
'Psychology and Human Resources'. All I wanted was to be
trained so I could help the homeless. So how can I study
this crap when I desperately need help myself?
(JIMMY *has come into the living-room.*)

JIMMY: Dad always told you, if you want to help the homeless,
you should go into the construction business.
(JIMMY *goes over to the radiator under the window. He puts his
hand on it and turns to his sisters in surprise.*)
It's warm!
(*The girls rush over. As the three press themselves against the
warm radiator, they see two hookers, one black and one blonde,
getting out of a car and wiggling their way towards the front
door.*

JIMMY *leers. His sisters shake their heads reprovingly. They
duck down so as not to be seen, pulling* JIMMY *with them.*

*The doorbell rings. The three of them remain sitting on the
floor.*)

CHLOE: (*Whispering*) I guess I'll have to prostitute myself.

JIMMY: Let's keep that as a last resort.

CHLOE: (*Hitting him*) My art, not my body. I'd better do that
stupid calendar for the insurance company.
(*They look at her with pity. The hookers give up and go back to
their car.* CHLOE *gets up, resolved, and exits.* JIMMY *follows
her out.*)

DAPHNE: You make me feel ashamed, Chloe. (*She looks at the
alien world beyond.*) I guess I should go out there and do
something too. (*She exits.*)

INT. HALLWAY. DAY
CHLOE *and* DAPHNE *are going up the stairs. They turn and stare at*
JIMMY.

JIMMY: Don't say it. Don't say it. I'm going . . . on bike . . .
find job . . . out door . . .
(*He grabs his bike and goes.*)

EXT. MESSENGER OFFICE. DAY

A group of messenger boys explode out of the doorway of a messenger office by the Brooklyn Bridge and speed down the road. JIMMY *pedals furiously among them.*

EXT. 7TH AVENUE. BUSY STREET. DAY

JIMMY, *wearing all the paraphernalia of a messenger boy, drives his bike through the busy traffic. He is exhausted from the day's work. Sweat shines on his pained face as he uses all his strength to pedal.*

EXT. OFFICE BUILDING. DAY

JIMMY *pulls into the kerb and falls off the bike exhausted. He chains the front wheel to a street lamp. As he staggers into the office building he pulls out a package from his messenger bag and drops it on to the reception desk, turns and staggers back to the street. His bike is gone. All that remains is the front wheel, still attached to the street lamp. He stares at it, too drained to respond. He turns and walks away like an old man. He lets the messenger bag slip from his shoulder to the pavement.*

EXT. SUPERMARKET. DAY

DAPHNE, *looking very pleased with herself, is pushing a cart loaded with cans and bottles. She wheels it into the supermarket.*

INT. SUPERMARKET. DAY

DAPHNE *stops at the machine that pays five cents a can or bottle. As she is about to feed it, a bag man blocks it with a can of his own.* DAPHNE *notices, to her shame, a line of bums, each with a market cart full of cans and bottles, waiting their turn.* DAPHNE *smiles apologetically and pushes her cart to the end of the line. They eye her suspiciously. She is moved by their plight, and embarrassed to be there. An old bag lady ahead of her has pitifully few cans in her basket. She eyes Daphne's cart sadly. Impulsively,* DAPHNE *takes an armful of her cans and bottles and deposits them in the bag lady's cart.*

DAPHNE: Here. I've got plenty.

> (*The bums stare at her. She struggles to keep her composure. She is close to tears. Finally, she abandons her cart and flees.*)

INT. LIVING-ROOM. DUTCH HOUSE. DAY

DAPHNE *is sitting in a chair, staring blankly at the Manet painting, which is propped up against the wall.* CHLOE *is starting to paint a*

mural on the wall. JIMMY *is in the conservatory, fiddling with the computer equipment that he has installed there. He is programming an image of a collapsing building. It looks like the Taj Mahal. A little man is trying to escape the destruction. Each time Jimmy's adjustments make it look more convincing. He is so absorbed that his limbs jerk in sympathy with the movements on the screen. He leaps up, crumples, hops, stamps his feet, convulses. He improvises sound effects – explosions, whistles, bleeps. He seems to be having a frustrating time of it. He hears the front doorbell ring. When he looks into the living-room he sees* CHLOE *bringing in two* DELIVERY MEN *weighed down with paints, brushes and packages of other artists' materials.*

1ST DELIVERY MAN: That's a lot of paint, lady.

(JIMMY *enters the living-room as the* DELIVERY MEN *leave.*)

JIMMY: (*Looking at the paint*) Sure is. (*He grabs the money jar and sees that it is almost empty.*) You blew the last of our money!

CHLOE: I can't paint without paint and I only get paid when I deliver the calendar, which is twelve large paintings away.

JIMMY: OK. We're out of money. No one in their right mind is going to rent a room in this rat hole. Here's what we have to do. Each of us has got to find a friend and talk him into boarding with us.

CHLOE: Right.

JIMMY: Right. Right now. (*He exits.*)

INT. STOCKBROKERS' OFFICE. DAY

A large area is filled with rows of desks, each with a computer screen. Everybody is on the phone. Most of them are on two. The brokers shout and wave bits of paper. Runners fly up and down between the desks, snatching the paper from the waving hands and dropping others on to desks.

JIMMY dodges his way through the chaos, looking for TOM. *He finds him at his desk and on the phone.* JIMMY *spins* TOM *around on his swivel chair. The telephone cord is almost strangling* TOM, *but he continues to shout into the phone. He kicks and thumps* JIMMY, *but to no avail.*

TOM: American Demolition? Yeah, yeah, I'll look into it. The timing's right. The stock is way down, after that Dutch House disaster.

> (TOM *hangs up, then takes back the receiver and hits* JIMMY *with it. Holding it in the air, he swivels round on his chair, untangling himself from the cord.*)

A client of ours wants to raid your father's company.

JIMMY: I want you to rent a room in our place.

TOM: In that slum?

JIMMY: You told me your step-mother wants you out of the house.

TOM: Yeah, but I was thinking of a penthouse, not a flophouse.

JIMMY: Your room will be right next to Chloe's.

> (TOM *raises an eyebrow. The phone rings and he answers it.*)

TOM: (*To* JIMMY) I'll take it. (*Into phone*) No. Not you. Not at that price.

EXT. BROWNSTONE HOUSE. DAY

DAPHNE *thumps her fists against the front door.*

DAPHNE: (*Shouting*) Let me in! I hate it there! I want to come home!

INT. DINING-ROOM ON GROUND FLOOR. DAY

JEAN *and* STEWART *sit at the large dining-room table.* STEWART *eats heartily, his newspaper propped up before him.* JEAN *stiffens as she hears* DAPHNE's *cries.* STEWART *shakes his head sternly in answer to her pleading eyes.*

DAPHNE: (*Voice over*) Mommy, please! I haven't eaten properly for days. Jimmy's lost his bike. I'm losing my mind.

STEWART: (*Taking another mouthful*) Be strong, Jean. It's the only way they'll learn.

DAPHNE: (*Voice over, plaintively*) Daddy, Daddy, please let me in. I love you.

(STEWART *winces when he hears her call to him.* JEAN *stands.*)

JEAN: Coffee.

(JEAN *goes into the kitchen with Stewart's cup. He is watching her out of the corner of his eye. When she is in the kitchen, she puts down the cup and makes a dash for the door.* STEWART *leaps after her.*)

INT. ENTRANCE HALLWAY AND STAIRS. DAY

JEAN *flies into the hall, but is intercepted by* STEWART *as she nears the door. She struggles forward, but he blocks her path, forcing her to climb his back, but to no avail. He throws her off into the living-room.* JOSE *and his wife, the cook, watch impassively from the back of the hallway.*

EXT. BROWNSTONE HOUSE. DAY

JEAN *appears at a lower window. She sends* DAPHNE *mute signals of her helplessness and sympathy. The letter box opens, revealing* STEWART's *eyes inches away from* DAPHNE's.

STEWART: (*An emotional whisper*) Daphne, my baby, this hurts me worse than it hurts you.

DAPHNE: If that were true, you'd be screaming in agony.

(DAPHNE *kicks the door and turns away, running down the steps and jumping on top of the bonnet of the limousine, making a spectacle of herself to embarrass her parents.*)

EXT. BROOKLYN BRIDGE WALKWAY. DUSK

CHLOE, LIONEL *and two* INDIAN WOMEN *in saris traipse across the walkway in procession.* CHLOE *is pushing a rack of clothes on casters. She has difficulty in keeping it on a straight course.* LIONEL *is pushing a cart containing half a dozen tailor's dummies and bolts of cloth. One of the* INDIAN WOMEN *pushes an old pram with two sewing machines in it, while the other steadies them.*

LIONEL: (*Frustrated*) Why did I let you charm me into this?

CHLOE: (*Feebly*) Don't forget it's a Landmark now. Maybe you could put it on your label – you know, like a French château wine.

LIONEL: Nothing but mud and ruins. Who's going to take me

seriously in a dump like that?

CHLOE: I would. Well, I would if I didn't know you so well.

> (LIONEL *is wearing a stylish, wide-brimmed hat. He pulls it off and throws it off the bridge.*)

LIONEL: That hat's a Manhattan hat. I can't wear it over there.

EXT. UNDER BROOKLYN BRIDGE. DUSK

The hat floats down. A decrepit-looking STREET BUM *sees it descending and chases it with surprising agility. He catches it neatly and puts it on his head. He finds himself standing next to* DAPHNE, *who contemplates the flowing water of the Hudson. She looks as if she is about to throw herself in.*

BUM: (*Southern accent*) Do it, if you're going to do it! I can't stand the suspense!

> (DAPHNE *turns and sees the* BUM *looking at her with a mocking smile.*)

DAPHNE: (*Haughtily*) I'm waiting for the tide. I don't want to wade through that smelly mud, do I?

BUM: You can always jump off the bridge.

DAPHNE: (*Angrily*) No, I can't. I'm scared of heights.

BUM: If it's for love, don't do it. The pain is bad but it only lasts between twelve and fourteen days. Believe me.

DAPHNE: (*Shaking her head*) I'm punishing my parents.

BUM: (*He gets it and smiles*) Make sure there's someone reliable around to fish you out.

> (*He shakes his head and turns away.* DAPHNE *watches him join a small group of down-and-outs huddled around a fire under an arch of the bridge. She looks about her and, for the first time, sees this sad, cold place where the homeless live, rows of cardboard boxes as their shelter. Concerned for them, she forgets about herself. She walks towards the little group. The* BUM *is doing conjuring tricks for his uninterested audience. He appears to pluck from thin air lightweight supermarket bags, which float up into the sky like balloons.* DAPHNE *applauds, delighted. Suicide has slipped her mind.*)

DAPHNE: You're a magician.

BUM: A lifetime of deceit.

> (*Daphne's face lights up with a joyful notion. She plucks up courage.*)

DAPHNE: Look, I have to find a friend to live in our house. Well,

I only have one friend and I don't think she likes me right now. I wonder, sir, would you teach me magic if . . . ?
(*The* BUM *eyes her shrewdly. He is amused.*)

INT. DUTCH HOUSE. DAY
The house is now full and the family and their lodgers go about their business in their separate rooms. CHLOE *is painting a winter landscape on to the wall of her room.* TOM, *in his tiny bedroom next door to Chloe's, is getting dressed. His suits and shirts hang from clothes lines stretched across the room. It is so confined that he has trouble tying his bow tie.* LIONEL *is in his workroom, where he also sleeps, draping and shaping material on a model,* OLIVIA. *She is reading a biography of Oscar Wilde and slowly moving to the music playing in the room. This causes* LIONEL *to have difficulties in pinning the hem of her skirt and he slaps her leg to get her to stand still.*

DAPHNE *is listening to very loud music in her bedroom. She moves restlessly but rhythmically around the room, getting dressed and gathering up her schoolbooks. She goes out of her room into the hall. She opens the door to Tom's room, where he is in the final stages of tying his bow tie. She says good morning to him and then moves down the hall past Chloe's room. Through the open doorway she sees* CHLOE *painting.* CHLOE *pays no attention to* DAPHNE, *who moves on down the hall past the toilet. She rattles the handle and says good morning to the* BUM, *who is sitting contentedly on the toilet reading the* New York Times.

Jimmy's bed is in the conservatory and he has set up his computer near it, half hidden by the foliage. He taps at the keyboard, programming his video game, but in an urgent need to pee he finally tears himself away and runs up the stairs and past the two INDIAN WOMEN *working at sewing machines on the upper landing. He tries the bathroom door, which is locked. He rattles it irritably. He turns away and speeds back the way he came, but trips on a swathe of cloth and, twisted in it, tumbles half-way down the stairs.*

LIONEL, *hearing his cries, appears on the landing beside the* INDIAN WOMEN. DAPHNE *and* CHLOE *come out of their rooms as* JIMMY *picks himself up and snarls at* LIONEL.
JIMMY: You never said we'd have Bang-fucking-kok in the hallway!

23

LIONEL: That's an unprovoked racist slur.

PURNA: Excuse me. We're from Bom-fucking-bay.

CHLOE: This has nothing to do with Purna and Mya. They don't live here.

JIMMY: OK. Let's zero in on the rent.

DAPHNE: Anyway, fashion is bad ecology. It makes us hate what we are wearing and buy things we don't want.

(*The* BUM *from Brooklyn Bridge appears from the bathroom, holding the* New York Times.)

BUM: At my age, I need an hour in the bathroom in the morning, and there's always one of them skinny, titless mannequins in there, fluffing up her hair.

(*Everybody turns and glares at the* BUM.)

JIMMY: (*Running for the toilet*) Start paying your rent, you can shit all day.

DAPHNE (*Following* JIMMY *to the toilet, followed by* LIONEL) He'll pay once he's worked up his magic act. I'm trying to get him some engagements right now.

(*The* BUM *winces at the prospect.*)

LIONEL: (*Shutting the door of the toilet*) You're so ungrateful. I've given you seven and a half per cent of my couture business.

JIMMY: (*Voice over*) Seven and a half per cent of zip is zilch.

LIONEL: You all agreed I could defer my rent for two months, until the collection is ready.

JIMMY: (*Opening the door of the toilet and coming out*) The only tenant who comes across around here is my friend Tom!

(*Right on cue,* TOM *appears, immaculately dressed. He goes past them on the stairs, ignoring the rumpus.*)

CHLOE: He doesn't have to be so smug about it. Do you, Tom?

TOM: Oh yes, I do.

JIMMY: We're broke. We're desperate. The Fag doesn't pay. The Shit doesn't pay . . .

CHLOE: (*Furious*) Don't call him The Fag.

DAPHNE: Don't call him The Shit.

BUM: (*Drawing himself up with dignity*) At least I'm *The* Shit. You're just *a* shit.

(LIONEL *strides over to* JIMMY *and pins him with a venomous look.*)

LIONEL: And this is your contribution? The slum landlord

harassing tenants?

JIMMY: When I sell my video game . . .

(LIONEL *and the others laugh derisively.*)

SHERYL: (*Point of view*) Hi! Sheryl Corman, I'm here about the
room.

(*The crazed faces freeze, then smile sweetly as they turn to greet
the newcomer. At the bottom of the stairs is a very pretty girl.*
THE SHIT *takes in Sheryl's designer clothes and comes forward
with a crafty smirk on his face.* JIMMY *is dumbstruck by Sheryl's
Californian glow.*)

THE SHIT: Ah, yes. Well, you better know right off. This
establishment only accepts cash. Three months in advance.
We have official Landmark Status.

JIMMY: What are you talking about, three months in advance?

SHERYL: I don't care. Six months if you like. (*Looking about her*)
The Karma here is major. Fifteen people achieved
Glossolalia in this house in 1935.

JIMMY: Glosso what?

SHERYL: Glossolalia, speaking in tongues. I'm researching it for
my Masters': 'The Paranormal in Religion'.

25

INT. LIVING-ROOM/CONSERVATORY. NIGHT

A party is in full swing. THE SHIT *is teaching* LIONEL *the tango.*
OLIVIA *is practising on her own.* TOM *is leaning drunkenly on the*
fireplace, ogling CHLOE, *who is dancing with* DAPHNE. JIMMY *is*
attempting the tango with SHERYL, *besotted with her.*

SHERYL: I'm getting in touch at so many levels. It's awesome.
This house just vibrates with the most amazing frequencies.
Can't you feel it?

JIMMY: Every time I touch you I feel it.

> (TOM *staggers over to where* CHLOE *and* DAPHNE *are dancing*
> *together.* THE SHIT *leaves* LIONEL *by the fireplace and dances*
> *off with* OLIVIA. TOM *has reached* DAPHNE *and turns her*
> *around, thinking that she is* CHLOE.)

TOM: I thought you were Chloe.

DAPHNE: Sisters. We're the same . . . but different.

TOM: Different? In what way?

DAPHNE: You'll have to find out for yourself, won't you?

> (TOM *smiles nervously. They dance.* JIMMY *is showing his*
> *computer gear to* SHERYL.)

JIMMY: This is the real nervous system of the planet. My brain is

connected to half the world through this, just by plugging in and punching keys. (*He leans towards her, snakily.*) We're doing the same thing. It's just our equipment that's different. (*She slips from under him as he tries to kiss her.*)

SHERYL: Let's keep it cerebral, shall we?

(*He pretends to beat his head against the wall in a paroxysm of sexual frustration.*

Later, TOM *has passed out and is lying against Chloe's mural of a Matisse painting.* CHLOE *passes him on her way into the kitchen with some dirty dishes.* JIMMY *and* LIONEL *are washing up.* THE SHIT *sits slumped over the table.*)

CHLOE: (*Sighing*) Well, we made the most of Sheryl's rent. Bills all paid and just enough left over for this decadent celebration.

THE SHIT: A brief pause on the road to damnation.

JIMMY: Broke again and can't get laid.

LIONEL: If we can somehow stay afloat for a month, till Chloe and I finish our projects . . .

DAPHNE: (*Coming into the kitchen*) There is a way out of this nightmare and you know it, Jimmy.

JIMMY: (*Panic-stricken*) No.

CHLOE: You'll have to sell your soul to save your sisters.
    (*Both sisters eye their brother.* JIMMY *groans.*)
JIMMY: Work for Dad? Never.

INT. STEWART'S OUTER OFFICE. DAY
JIMMY *comes into the outer office, where the girls sitting at their computer screens greet him cheerily. It is a big open office. At the far end, separated by a glass wall,* STEWART *can be seen pacing up and down his private office.* JIMMY *approaches his father's* SECRETARY, *keeping an eye on his father, who waves his fists, points accusing fingers and rants, soundlessly. He gives her a peck on the cheek.*
JIMMY: (*Nervously*) How's the great dictator?
SECRETARY: (*Cheerfully*) Dictating. I think it's a letter to the *New York Times.*
JIMMY: Can you sneak me in?
SECRETARY: (*Glancing at her watch*) Well, a couple of minutes. We're expecting the real estate developers who are supposed to buy the Dutch House site from us. He's going to try to convince them to build around it.

INT. STEWART'S OFFICE. DAY
STEWART *is declaiming into the dictating machine.*
STEWART: This perverse passion for preservation, for pickling

the past, for turning this city into a museum is . . . is . . .
(*He looks up as* JIMMY *puts his head around the door.*)
Jimmy, what brings you here?
(JIMMY *steps in and opens his arms in a gesture of surrender.*)
JIMMY: (*Nervous*) Dad, I've been doing some serious thinking.
I'd like to come back and work for you.
STEWART: (*Sarcastically*) Oh, you've suddenly discovered a
passion for demolition.
JIMMY: Well, I like bulldozers, Dad. But I'm still not in love with
them.
STEWART: So what do you have to offer?
JIMMY: I'll computerize the business. You know, modernize the
place.
STEWART: I've got computers coming out of my ears.
JIMMY: Yeah, Dad, but you don't love them, you just put up
with them.
(STEWART *smiles, acknowledging Jimmy's point. He looks
tenderly at his son for a moment, then shakes his head sceptically.
He waves* JIMMY *away.*)
STEWART: Your sisters put you up to this?
JIMMY: (*Looking embarrassed*) Kind of . . .
STEWART: Nice try, but sorry. Was there something else?
(JIMMY *starts to leave, then turns with a new idea.*)
JIMMY: Challenge you to Slap.
STEWART: What?
JIMMY: Slap. If I win, I get a job . . . Slap.
STEWART: Jimmy, please.
JIMMY: Slap. Come on.
STEWART: You've never won yet.
JIMMY: There will come a time. It could be now.
(STEWART *shakes his head dismissively.*)
JIMMY: You're getting old.
STEWART: I'm getting old?
(STEWART *gets up, provoked.*)
JIMMY: Come on.
(STEWART *moves over to* JIMMY. *They stand opposite each
other, bracing themselves, legs spread, hands raised, palms
outwards. It is obviously a game they have played over the years.
The purpose is to unbalance the opponent, either by slapping his
hands and forcing him backwards by sheer strength or by*

withdrawing your hands as he strikes so that he topples forward, carried by his own weight. They clash full force. Neither budges. Then follows a series of false moves and feinting. Their eyes are locked together, they know each other's game. The desk buzzer sounds but STEWART *ignores it, concentrating on the contest. He smiles, which angers* JIMMY. *Jimmy lunges at* STEWART's *palms.* STEWART *pulls them away, causing* JIMMY *to fall forward. He tries to regain his balance by windmilling his arms, but topples to defeat. As* STEWART *turns away, quietly triumphant, he locks eyes with the two real-estate developers, who have been watching, appalled, through the glass. Behind them, looking dismayed, are* HAMILTON, *the banker, and* HARRY.)

INT. LIVING-ROOM/CONSERVATORY. DAY
DAPHNE, *comes in carrying her schoolbooks.* CHLOE *is painting a seascape on to the wall.* DAPHNE *inspects it.*
DAPHNE: (*Seeking attention*) Chloe! Chloe!
CHLOE: (*Without looking up*) Go away and play.
   (DAPHNE *wanders into the conservatory.* TOM *and* JIMMY *are working on a tangled complex of computers. They both peer at a small screen, their heads almost touching. They type on to the keyboard. They laugh, then concentrate on the screen again.*

DAPHNE *sighs loudly from the doorway. Sensing her presence,*
they tear their heads away from the screen.)
TOM *and* JIMMY: Hi! Hello, Daph.
DAPHNE: Don't call me Daph! Do I look like a Daph?
(*She smiles at* TOM.)
You can call me Daph, Tom.
TOM: Jimmy's got a great new game coming along here. Check this
out.
(DAPHNE *goes to them, leaning down between their heads. But*
instead of looking at the screen, she eyes TOM *admiringly.* TOM's
gaze drifts over to CHLOE.)
DAPHNE: What about Dad?
JIMMY: I tried. I tried. I fell on my face.
DAPHNE: (*Moaning*) That's terrible. It's terminal. No money.
We're non-people.
JIMMY: We don't need Dad. I've sold Tom a piece of my new game –
for cash. We can all survive on that for a while.
TOM: (*Looking sheepish*) If I can get hooked on it, I figure there must
be a million like minded idiots out there dying for the same fix.
(TOM *reaches forward and presses the keyboard. The stock-market*
prices come up.)
Let's see how the market's doing. That's a much easier game
to play and everybody wins. Well, nearly everybody.
DAPHNE: (*Raising her voice*) All you boys think about is playing
games on a computer when the real world is falling apart
around us.
(TOM *and* JIMMY *blink at her, uncomprehending as* DAPHNE
switches the screen back to the video game, picks up the joy stick
and manically begins to play the game.)

EXT. DEMOLITION SITE. DAY
STEWART *is setting his detonating equipment high up in a new office*
block that is under construction. It is raw concrete and the window a
bare, glassless hole which gives a view down on to a huge building he is
preparing to demolish. A police officer is scanning the site with
binoculars. He confers by walkie-talkie with his colleagues on the
ground, who are ensuring the evacuation of the area. The FOREMAN *is*
by the detonating device.
FOREMAN: Section one, clear. Section two, clear. Section three,
clear.

STEWART: Arming.

FOREMAN: Arming detonator.

(HARRY *appears, breathless and agitated.*)

HARRY: Stewart! News!

STEWART: The Dutch House?

HARRY: No. Better. Bona fide take-over bid! A raider. They're offering our stockholders twenty per cent over the current market price.

STEWART: That's all I need. A proxy fight.

HARRY: We've got to consider it, with so many of your assets tied up in that Dutch House site.

STEWART: (*Angry*) Those bastards, those Wall Street, wise-ass bastards. They come in, buy up a business, kick out the professionals who built it up, sell off the assets and leave it in ruins. I'm telling you, capitalism is in the toilet.

(STEWART *gets the all-clear signal from the police officer. He turns to the* FOREMAN.)

All clear.

FOREMAN: (*Into walkie-talkie*) All sections clear.

HARRY: Obviously we're obliged to notify the stockholders of the offer.

STEWART: I'll buy back the stock myself if I have to.

HARRY: You don't have that kind of money.

(STEWART *raises an arm. The police officer nods assent. A warning signal sounds.*)

STEWART: (*Eyes on his watch*) I'll raise the money. No one is going to destroy what I've built up.

(*To* FOREMAN)

Firing.

FOREMAN: (*To walkie-talkie*) Firing.

(STEWART *pushes a series of buttons. The building crumbles in on itself.*)

STEWART: Poetry. Pure poetry.

(HARRY *nods agreement.*

Dust settles on STEWART *and* HARRY.)

DAPHNE: (*Voice over*) I think I take after Dad. I always have these great urges to destroy things.

INT. DUTCH HOUSE. CHLOE'S ROOM. DAY

CHLOE *is preparing* DAPHNE *for one of the 'live paintings' that she has been commissioned to do for the calendar.* DAPHNE *stands against a backdrop painted in* trompe l'œil. CHLOE *paints on* DAPHNE'S *naked body so that it becomes part of the scene behind her. Her face is an inch from* DAPHNE'S.

DAPHNE: You think it's hereditary?

CHLOE: Hmmm?

DAPHNE: Is it genetic? These destructive impulses?

> (CHLOE *looks through her camera. She returns to* DAPHNE. *The 'live painting' gives the illusion that the walls of the room are collapsing, revealing a strange winter landscape beyond.*)
> Why am I January? Why can't I be June? (*Pause for answer*) Do I look cold and bleak? That's it, isn't it? That's what freezes out all the boys?

CHLOE: Hmmm?

DAPHNE: (*Flaring up*) I'm glad I'm not you, Chloe. I'd bore myself to death!

CHLOE: You're definitely January, Daphne. Perfect.

> (CHLOE *clicks the camera, catching the haughty, angry expression on Daphne's face as* LIONEL *comes through the door.*)

LIONEL: A bit risqué for an insurance company calendar, isn't it?

CHLOE: It's a risk I'll have to take. You can't take out insurance against failure in art.

LIONEL: (*With unconvincing bravado*) I never consider the possibility of failure.

CHLOE: (*Shrewdly*) You're stuck, aren't you?

LIONEL: Me, stuck . . . ? (*Then feebly*) I guess I am.

INT. LIONEL'S WORKROOM. DAY

The room is covered in swatches of cloth and half-dressed dummies. There are rolls of material hanging from long metal pipes that stretch the length of the walls. LIONEL *is at a drawing-board, showing his sketches to* CHLOE *and* DAPHNE, *who is still dressed in her 'live painting' gear and body make-up.*

DAPHNE: (*Making an effort*) Hmm. Lovely. Wonderful. Oh, beautiful.

(CHLOE *studies them seriously and silently.* LIONEL *watches them anxiously.*)

LIONEL: (*Quickly, fishing*) I did those today. Roughs really. Just scratches.

(*They are highly finished and look like they involved a lot of work.*)

DAPHNE: Yes, I suppose they are.

LIONEL: Suppose they're what?

DAPHNE: Roughs. Scratches. But lovely scratches.

LIONEL: (*Grasping at straws*) Really?

(*He turns to* CHLOE, *anxiously awaiting her opinion.*)

CHLOE: (*Kindly*) Just a little bit Joan Collinsy.

LIONEL: What do you mean, Joan Collinsy? What do you know about fashion?

DAPHNE: (*Encouragingly*) They would look lovely on our mother, Lionel.

LIONEL: That's very hurtful and not at all helpful.

(DAPHNE *flares up, but manages to bite her tongue. She goes out, shrugging.*)

Why's she so touchy?

(CHLOE *puts her arms around him and looks at the drawings over his shoulder.*)

CHLOE: (*Gently*) I never told you this but I thought your show

34

was so amazing. You're an original. You've got to make what you like, not what you think other people like. Don't you think?

LIONEL: (*Smiling*) I can't think when you're smothering me like this!

INT. THE SHIT'S BEDROOM. DAY
DAPHNE *enters the room, holding a cup of coffee.* THE SHIT *is lying under a pile of covers. The place is a litter of dirty cups and glasses, clothes and newspapers.*

DAPHNE: Shitty! Wake up. It's two o'clock. Here's a lovely cup of coffee.
(*He opens one eye and runs it over Daphne's body paint.*)

THE SHIT: Go back to your own planet. This one's all used up.
(*He takes the coffee, sighs and looks bleakly out of the window.*)
What's to get up for? Nothing but empty-brained idiots, spraying aerosol cans at their armpits, punching holes in the ozone layer. It looks like I just might live to see the end of the world. Nobody's going to miss us when we blow ourselves up.
(DAPHNE *rummages in The Shit's battered old trunk. It contains the accoutrements of his craft. She pulls out a shabby old tuxedo and brushes it down.*)

DAPHNE: We know all that. But while we're waiting for the end you have to find a way to pay your rent. You're a magician. You have a gift. And guess what? I've found you a little job. (THE SHIT *chokes on his coffee.*)

THE SHIT: I need at least another three months of rehearsals, Daphne, honey.

DAPHNE: (*Hard*) Oh no, you don't. You have an engagement.

INT. A NEW YORK APARTMENT. DAY

THE SHIT, *assisted by* DAPHNE, *stands before a children's party doing tricks. A live dove is turned into a roast pigeon. A bunch of flowers wilts. Some children play and fight, ignoring his efforts, others are immersed in a video game. Only one little boy stands very close, watching* THE SHIT *intently.*

THE SHIT: (*Bitterly*) What are you looking at?

INT. LIVING-ROOM/CONSERVATORY. DAY

CHLOE *paints* THE SHIT*'s body and the wall behind him. He watches her absently. She has painted a great, flooded landscape. The water appears to be cascading into the room.* THE SHIT *bestrides the fireplace, which has become incorporated in the design.*

THE SHIT: Nobody wants my old tricks any more. Your brother is the real magician of today, with that Pandora's Box of his.

INT. CONSERVATORY. DAY
JIMMY *is watering the tropical plants. They look a lot healthier than they did.*

THE SHIT *is sitting at Jimmy's computer screen, tapping away at the keyboard with one finger. He turns to* JIMMY, *a nasty crooked smile on his face.*
THE SHIT: James, I think I just hacked into that bank account of yours. Why don't I add a couple of zeros to your balance?
(JIMMY *dives at the computer and breaks the connection.*)
JIMMY: (*Furious*) Don't pervert *my* computer. It's pure. It's not all twisted and crooked like some old con-artist.
THE SHIT: So you admit I'm an artist.

INT. LIVING-ROOM. DAY
The evil smile remains on THE SHIT's *face but his eyes are full of prophecy. He is perched against the magical, flooded landscape. He is Merlin.*
THE SHIT: Floppy discs, mega-bytes, IBM-compatible. Mine eyes have seen the true magic of the age.
(CHLOE *takes her photo.*)
CHLOE: Got you.

INT. BROWNSTONE HOUSE. NIGHT
Jean and Stewart's house is silent and empty. STEWART *appears in the hallway, carrying a newspaper. He looks up the stairs, listens, then shakes his head. He returns to the drawing-room.*

INT. DRAWING-ROOM. NIGHT
STEWART: I guess it just takes a little time to get used to the silence.
(JEAN *is making photo-collages of each of her three children. She is cutting up snaps and pasting them together.*)
JEAN: I'll never get used to it.
STEWART: (*Sharply*) Peace at last. I don't miss them.
JEAN: You never really knew them, always working.
(STEWART *leans over her and flicks the pages of the photo album.*)
STEWART: What's this, then? Who's that?

(*He points to pictures of himself playing with his small children.*
JEAN *shakes her head and smiles to herself, infuriating*
STEWART. *He stares at her, challengingly.* JEAN *keeps her eyes
on the photos.*)

JEAN: (*Sighs*) I think we should peek in on them. See if they're all
right.

STEWART: Jean, stay away. They've got to do it on their own.
(*She sighs again. A deep silence falls over the house. He starts to
hyperventilate.*)
I've got enough pressure without your silent accusations. I
can't breathe in here. (*He storms from the room and the front
door slams.*)

EXT. DUTCH HOUSE. NIGHT
*A jeep drives up and stops across from the house. The headlights turn
off. Sitting at the wheel is* STEWART. *He looks across at the house,
with its lighted windows. There is a pained and uncertain expression
on his face. He starts to get out but hesitates.*

INT. HALLWAY. DUTCH HOUSE. NIGHT
STEWART *opens the door with his keys and slips silently into the house.*

He walks through the hall. Soft rock music is playing. Laughter and the hum of voices come from the living-room. He peers through the half-open door.

DAPHNE, JIMMY, CHLOE, TOM, LIONEL *and* OLIVIA (*the model*) *are all draped over the big, ugly second-hand sofas and armchairs in a variety of abandoned attitudes.* OLIVIA *is brushing* CHLOE'*s long hair. Jimmy's legs are propped up over the arm of the sofa, his feet moving to the music. The fire casts a soft light on the gathering. One of Chloe's bizarre landscapes dominates the wall behind them.*

THE SHIT, *holding an imaginary partner, dances across the room, executing a series of elaborate steps.*

CHLOE: (*Hugging* DAPHNE) It doesn't matter, Daphne. We have each other. Which is more than most people have.

DAPHNE: Most people wouldn't want us!

 (STEWART *is moved. He turns away, back to the front door. As he turns he realizes that* SHERYL *has been watching him from the front door. They look at each other for a moment. She can see that he is very disturbed.*)

SHERYL: (*Gently*) Who are you?

STEWART: (*After a pause*) A distant relative. (*He squirms past her and melts into the night.*)

INT. LIVING-ROOM/CONSERVATORY. NIGHT
SHERYL *enters the living-room and joins her friends.*
TOM: We almost have each other. Jimmy almost has Sheryl, I
    almost have Chloe.
    (*They all laugh at* TOM.)
CHLOE: Dream on, sweetheart.
    (TOM *looks crestfallen.*)
SHERYL: I think your father was here.
    (*Silence drops like a stone.*)

INT. TOM'S ROOM. DAY
A landscape covers the wall. CHLOE *touches part of the painting with her brush. It moves. It is* TOM. *He lifts his arm slightly, so that he emerges from the picture.* CHLOE *is painting his body so that it disappears into the wall.*
CHLOE: How do you know you're in love with me? What is it you
    like about me?
TOM: Come to think of it, I don't like anything about you. I'm
    just hopelessly in love with you.

(CHLOE, *absorbed suddenly with a painting problem, gives a cry of disgust.* TOM *looks shattered.*)

CHLOE: This isn't right.

TOM: (*Crestfallen*) Oh.

CHLOE: Can we try again tomorrow?

TOM: (*Brightening up*) Fine with me. I love it when your brush caresses my body.

EXT. TOM'S PORSCHE. DAY
The car speeds over the Brooklyn Bridge. TOM *is on the phone.*

TOM: Jimmy, it's ten-thirty.

JIMMY: (*Voice over*) I'm awake, I've been up for hours.

TOM: Patch into the Reuter feed. I'm out of touch.

INT. JIMMY'S BEDROOM IN CONSERVATORY. DAY
JIMMY *is under the bedcovers, trying to wake up. He leans over to his desk, where his computers stand. He clicks a button and the screen brightens.*

JIMMY: Yeah. OK.

41

INT. PORSCHE. DAY

TOM: Look at your father's stock. It was going through the roof when I left the office. I bought a bunch myself before the raiders moved in.

JIMMY: (*Voice over*) It just went up another point.

INT. STEWART AND JEAN'S BEDROOM. DAY

STEWART *and* JEAN *are getting ready to go out.* STEWART, *a telephone wedged between neck and shoulder, scrambles about the floor, looking for a stud button.*

STEWART: Up another point? We've got to buy quick.

JEAN: (*Pirouetting*) What do you think? Lionel designed it especially for me. Is it right for the White House?

STEWART: (*Banging his elbow as he hangs up*) Well, it's white. I guess it's right.

JEAN: (*Slumped down at her dressing-table*) Oh God. I feel so twitchy. Meeting the President.

STEWART: (*Rubbing his elbow*) Just be yourself.

JEAN: That's the last person I want to be.

(STEWART *grimaces and continues to search for the stud.* JEAN *powders her nose. There is a file of documents on the table before her.*)

I don't understand why you have to borrow money from the bank to buy back your own business. And now you want me to sell my beautiful house in Connecticut.

(*She picks up a silver-framed watercolour of her country house and gazes fondly at it.* STEWART *has finally found his stud and is struggling to get it in. He is breaking into a sweat. He speaks irritably.*)

I'm not selling the house. I'm only giving it as collateral. If worse comes to worst, I can always sell back the stock to pay the bank loan and redeem the deeds of the house.

(JEAN *flicks through the pages of the document, as though it has a bad smell.*)

JEAN: Bizarre, giving you this honour, just when everything's going wrong for you.

(STEWART *picks up a pen and shakes it at* JEAN.)

STEWART: I'm not going to argue with you. It's my money, I earned it, I bought that house for you.

JEAN: (*Taking the papers and pen*) And now you want it back.

STEWART: You got it.
JEAN: (*Pen suspended over the document, she looks up at him*)
Well . . . say you love me, then.

INT. TOM'S ROOM. DAY
Tom's painting is almost finished. CHLOE *has made him disappear completely. She goes to her camera.*
TOM: I love you . . .
CHLOE: Great. You've disappeared.
TOM: (*Feebly*) Help.

INT. WHITE HOUSE. DAY
A reception in a stateroom. STEWART *and* JEAN, *along with some thirty others, are gathered for a 'Captains of Industry' awards ceremony. A podium has been set up, displaying the handsome plaques to be presented. The press and TV are present.*

JEAN *looks out of the window at Pennsylvania Avenue and the monuments beyond, and then looks up proudly at her husband.*
PRESIDENTIAL AIDE: The President will be here momentarily.
When you shake his hand for the press photos, grasp it lightly. The President has a touch of tennis elbow.
(*This is greeted with good-humoured laughter.*

STEWART *is rehearsing with* JEAN *what he intends to tell the President . . .*)
STEWART: . . . and then I'm going to remind him that if we don't stay dynamic, we're dead. We've got to tear down the old and build up the new, like we always have. Somebody's got to tell him and I might be the guy to do it. Do you think he saw my letter in the *New York Times*?
(JEAN, *alarmed at his ranting, tries to humour him.*)
JEAN: Just say, 'Thanks, Mr President, it's a great honour.' Then he'll probably ask you how you got started in the demolition business.
STEWART: (*Grinning*) I blew up bridges in Korea, Mr President, and couldn't shake the habit.
(STEWART *laughs at his own joke.*)
JEAN: (*Sighs*) Well, why not? That always gets a laugh.
STEWART: (*Peeved*) What would you say, then?
JEAN: If I was receiving a medal? I richly deserve this, Mr

President. Twenty-five years trying to hold things together, while he destroyed everything around him, and finding out when the kids were gone that we had absolutely nothing to say to each other.

(*There are tears in Jean's eyes and her voice breaks.* STEWART *is alarmed, moved. He takes hold of her.*)

STEWART: Jean, sweetheart . . .

PRESIDENTIAL AIDE: (*Voice over*) Ladies and gentlemen, the President of the United States of America!

(*The band plays 'Hail to the Chief'.* STEWART *draws himself up stiffly to attention.* JEAN *sniffs and tries to hold back her tears.*)

INT. DUTCH HOUSE. KITCHEN. DAY

It is breakfast time. The whole household is in the kitchen, each person preparing his/her own fare. A TV set is perched on the icebox, playing a breakfast show. JIMMY *enters the kitchen, passing* SHERYL, *who is doing her Oriental breathing exercises. As he passes the TV he gives it a bang. He goes to the refrigerator, takes out a bar of chocolate and goes to the table.* DAPHNE *has been talking on the telephone about their parents' appearance on TV. She hangs up and gives the TV a thump as she passes it on her way over to the counter, where she begins slicing a melon.* CHLOE *is making toast.* THE SHIT *is staring into his tea.* TOM *is frying eggs and bacon at the stove. He dishes it out on to a plate and brings it over to the table, where his place is neatly laid out with a copy of the* Wall Street Journal. *As he sits down* JIMMY *knocks over a cup of coffee, which spills across the table.* JIMMY *quickly grabs a couple of slices of bread and soaks up the liquid with it like a sponge. The award ceremony comes on the television.* JIMMY *looks up.*

JIMMY: It's on!

(CHLOE *rushes towards the television to tune it in better.*)

CHLOE: How could he wear that tie with that suit?

LIONEL: That dress is so boring.

TOM: Don't knock it.

(*On the TV there is a close-up shot of* STEWART *as he approaches the podium.*)

JIMMY: C'mon Dad, you tell 'em!

THE SHIT: Every dog has his day.

DAPHNE: (*Shutting her eyes*) Ever since I became an anarchist, I refuse to look at politicians.

(STEWART *swallows, then mouths, 'Thank you, Mr President',*

44

and turns smartly away. There is a shot of teary-eyed JEAN.)

SHERYL: Your mother looks so proud and your father must be
out of his skull.

INT. BANK. DAY
STEWART *strides angrily through a big open office where lines of*
operatives tickle the keyboards of their VDUs. HARRY, *the lawyer, is*
in tow.
STEWART: I should never have gone public.
HARRY: It made you a paper millionaire.
STEWART: And what am I now? A paper tiger! (*He is furious. His*
anger is intimidating.)

INT. HAMILTON'S OFFICE. DAY
Stewart's fist hits the desk. In contrast to the high-tech outer area, the
office is leather and wood panel. STEWART *and* HARRY *have laid out*
documents on Hamilton's desk. HAMILTON *shakes his head*
regretfully.
STEWART: No! What do you mean, No? What happened to
loyalty?
HAMILTON: You can't get emotional about money, Stewart.
STEWART: Why not? Everybody else does. Most people today,
the only feelings they have are for money.

(STEWART *gestures to* HARRY *who draws another document from his briefcase as* STEWART *paces the room.*)

HARRY: Stewart's Brownstone, value three million dollars. Connecticut house, another one and a half, plus his twenty-nine per cent of American Demolition, plus, plus, plus.

(HAMILTON *joins* STEWART *at the window. They look across at the next building, where, at every window, computer serfs gaze at cathode-ray tubes.*)

HAMILTON: I'm just counselling you not to buy back your own stock, not while you're so . . . upset.

STEWART: You know the stock is undervalued, Hamilton. The property we have alone . . . which is why this prick is trying to steal it from me.

HAMILTON: Who knows what's going to happen to property values, Stewart?

STEWART: (*Exploding again*) You've got collateral coming out of your ass!

HAMILTON: The computer doesn't like the deal, Stewart.

STEWART: Who's running the bank, you or the little green numbers?

HAMILTON: They're getting the upper hand, Stewart. Computers.

(*His anxious eyes sweep over the view. Computer screens glow like alien eyes in every bay and window.*)

Impulses, flashing around the globe. We're just neurons in a big neurotic brain.

(*At a window in the building opposite is* TOM. *He looks up, startled to see* STEWART *staring at him.* STEWART *nods at* TOM. TOM *returns a nervous wave.*)

STEWART: You're losing your mind, Hamilton.

HAMILTON: *I'm* losing *my* mind?

STEWART: Just make the loan, Hamilton.

(HAMILTON *gives in and goes to his desk.* HARRY *is disturbed by Stewart's crazed manner.*)

HAMILTON: I must be.

INT. TOM'S OFFICE. DAY

TOM *sits at his desk watching* STEWART *and the banker,* HAMILTON. *He reaches across to the desk of his neighbour,* EDGAR, *and grabs a pair of binoculars, raising them to his eyes.*

46

TOM: Jesus! I can't believe my luck!
  (EDGAR *tries to grab the binoculars from him.*)
EDGAR: What's she doing? What's she doing?

VIEW THROUGH BINOCULARS
HAMILTON *signs a paper and hands it to* STEWART.

INT. TOM'S OFFICE. DAY
TOM *taps out a telephone number on the computer system on his desk,
still peering through the binoculars.*

VIEW THROUGH BINOCULARS
STEWART, HAMILTON *and* HARRY *are all talking urgently into
different phones and gesticulating.* TOM *focuses the binoculars on*
STEWART *and correctly interprets the phrase that* STEWART *is
repeating.*
TOM: (*Synchronizing with* STEWART) Buy American Demolition
  . . . American Demolition . . . Buy it. (*He dials a number and
  talks into the phone.*) Buy me one thousand. I've got a feeling
  they're going north again . . . Sure, I'll find the money.

INT. NEW YORK STOCK EXCHANGE. DAY
A DEALER, *arm stretched high, waves a paper.*
DEALER: American Demolition. I'm buying.
  (*Other dealers surge from all quarters, clamouring to sell and buy
  American Demolition, like dogs fighting over a bone.*)

EXT. DUTCH HOUSE. DAY
A bunch of stray dogs are fighting. DAPHNE, *coming home from
school, her books under her arm, breaks up the scrap.*
DAPHNE: Remember, you're animals. Stop behaving like human
  beings. (*She goes into the house.*)

INT. TOM'S OFFICE. DAY
With the phone glued to his ear, TOM *watches American Demolition
stock going higher and higher.* EDGAR, *on the phone, signals across to
him.*
EDGAR: (*Covering the mouthpiece*) Tom, Stewart's still slugging it
  out with the raider.

TOM: (*Shaking his head*) Is he mega-stubborn.

(EDGAR *raises a hand in warning*.)

EDGAR: (*Whispering*) Hey! Tom, the raider's getting ready to unload. You better be quick.

TOM: (*Into phone*) Sell! . . . Yeah, American Demolition. Yes, all of it.

(TOM *and* EDGAR *cheer and hug*.)

INT. LIVING-ROOM. DUTCH HOUSE. DAY

JIMMY *is dressed as Cupid. A pair of wings flop against his back.*
CHLOE *wires a halo to his head. Behind him is an oversize nude
painting of* SHERYL. JIMMY *has a pocket calculator in his hand. He
taps the keys and grimaces.*

JIMMY: Another three weeks before Lionel finishes his collection. How long to go on the calendar?

CHLOE: About the same.

JIMMY: We'll never make it on what we've got. People can tell when you don't have money. They look at you as if you smell bad.

CHLOE: And it's not only what it can buy. Just having it is sexy. Even Tom . . .

JIMMY: (*Eyeing her shrewdly*) Is he getting to you?

CHLOE: Well . . .

JIMMY:Let me drop a hint, then I can raise his rent.

CHLOE: Don't you dare. If he even suspected he'd be totally
unbearable.

INT. HALLWAY. DAY

SHERYL *enters the house, followed by a young black man,* MARCUS.
She looks into the living-room and sees JIMMY *dressed as Cupid.*

SHERYL: You look just darling!

(MARCUS *looks appreciatively at the nude painting of* SHERYL.)

MARCUS: (*To* SHERYL) So do you!

(*They start to go up the stairs.*)

INT. LIVING-ROOM. DAY

JIMMY, *stung with jealousy, flies after them.*

JIMMY: (*To* SHERYL) Sheryl! (*To* CHLOE) Hold on a second. (*He
gets down from his perch and goes up the stairs after* SHERYL.)

CHLOE: Don't do anything nasty while you're wearing that halo!

INT. UPSTAIRS HALL. DAY

SHERYL *and* MARCUS *disappear into Sheryl's bedroom, just as*
JIMMY *appears at the end of the hallway. He tiptoes towards her
door.* LIONEL *and* OLIVIA *come out of Lionel's workroom, giggling
at Jimmy's appearance.* JIMMY *comes up to Sheryl's door and puts
his ear to it. Strange, sexual noises come from it.* JIMMY *turns away,
despondent.*

As JIMMY *is walking away from Sheryl's room, he sees* DAPHNE
carrying a tray of coffee, and THE SHIT, *wearing his long underwear
and dragging chains and padlocks behind him.*

THE SHIT: (*Listlessly*) I'm growing weary of these chains, Daphne.

DAPHNE: Don't lose heart, Shitty. If you get this number down, we
can take it to Vegas. (*To* JIMMY) Is Sheryl back?

(DAPHNE *strides off towards Sheryl's room.* JIMMY *speeds after
her. The cries from the room sound even more passionate.* DAPHNE
bumps the door open with her hip and bursts in. JIMMY *anguished,
sticks his head round the opening.*

INT. SHERYL'S ROOM. DAY

SHERYL *holds a microphone to Marcus's lip. He seems to be in a deep trance, his body beating up and down. Sweat pours down his face and his shiny chest.* JIMMY *is relieved.*

DAPHNE: Coffee, Sheryl?

(SHERYL *shakes her head.* DAPHNE *approaches* MARCUS.)

DAPHNE: Coffee?

(*He beats his body forward, jolting his head up and down, as though in affirmation.*)

Sugar?

(*He makes the same movement.* DAPHNE *drops two lumps into his cup.*)

SHERYL: Is anybody there?

MARCUS: Who's asking?

SHERYL: Sheryl Corman.

MARCUS: Why does she ask?

SHERYL: It's for my Master's on the Paranormal. People talked in tongues in this house. See if you can reach one of them.

(DAPHNE *and* JIMMY *watch, wide-eyed.*)

MARCUS: (*Snapping out of his trance*) It's no good, I just can't get it on.

SHERYL: Are you taking me for a ride?

MARCUS: (*Leering*) I wouldn't mind.

(*He laughs goodnaturedly.* SHERYL *is amused despite herself.*)

INT. 'LIVE PAINTING' ROOM. DUTCH HOUSE. DAY

JIMMY *hops up on to the step disguised as a little cloud, from which he can point his arrow at* SHERYL'S *heart.*

JIMMY: I thought they were . . . but they weren't. They were just talking in tongues.

CHLOE: (*Amused*) Point the arrow at her heart.

(JIMMY *aims his arrow at* SHERYL'S *heart.*

TOM *enters the house. On his way upstairs he catches sight of* JIMMY *perched on his cloud. He immediately bursts into laughter.* JIMMY *turns and gives him the finger.*)

TOM: (*To* CHLOE) Looks good, looks good.

(CHLOE *looks at* TOM *dismissively. As he goes upstairs he bumps into* THE SHIT.)

THE SHIT: Ah, Tom, will you padlock my chains?

TOM: (*Striding up the stairs*) Not right now. I've got to make a call before the market closes.

THE SHIT: American Demolition still collapsing?

TOM: (*Smugly*) It's in ruins! Boy, did I bale out at the right time.
(THE SHIT *watches* TOM *go, then drags himself over to* CHLOE, *but when he sees* JIMMY *he bursts out laughing.* JIMMY *threatens* THE SHIT *with his arrow, then resumes his position.* CHLOE *ignores* THE SHIT *and snaps the picture.* THE SHIT *moves back upstairs.*)

INT. BATHROOM. DAY
Lionel's model, OLIVIA, *is removing her dress.* THE SHIT *enters. He offers his back to her, looking over his shoulder.*
THE SHIT: Olivia, will you chain me real tight?
OLIVIA: (*Closing the bathroom door*) I'm much better with a whip.
THE SHIT: (*Grinning evilly*) You little vixen.
(DAPHNE *enters.*)
DAPHNE: I'll do it, Olivia.

INT. LANDING. DAY
THE SHIT *is now chained up.* DAPHNE *places the padlock key between his teeth. He takes a deep breath and ducks under in the glass tank filled with water which stands on the landing. Underwater he starts to wriggle out of the chains.* DAPHNE *watches him anxiously.*

The doorbell rings. DAPHNE *skips down the stairs and opens the front door. A bedraggled, weeping* JEAN *stands in the doorway. She keeps her finger pressed to the doorbell. The continuous peal has brought the rest of the household to the door.*
DAPHNE: (*Trying to pry her mother's finger from the buzzer*) Now, Mother, we don't want to get a cramp in the finger.
(JEAN *is rigid, every muscle frozen.* JIMMY *and* CHLOE *peer out from the living-room.* TOM *and* LIONEL *appear from their rooms.* DAPHNE *gets a whiff of her mother's breath and looks wide-eyed at the others.* TOM *comes forward, hesitates, then slaps* JEAN *across the face.* JEAN *crumples into his arms and sobs.*)
CHLOE: (*Hitting* TOM) How dare you hit my mother. How dare you!
TOM: (*Hurt*) That's what you do for hysteria. That's what you do.
(*Everybody crowds around, trying to comfort* JEAN.)

INT. LANDING TANK. DAY
THE SHIT *still wriggles in the tank. He is banging his head against*

51

the wall of the tank. Now and again he mouths the word 'Help'. The key is no longer in his mouth.

INT. KITCHEN. DAY
The members of the household are all assembled. JIMMY, DAPHNE, CHLOE, LIONEL *and* SHERYL, *who is sitting in a yoga position, meditating.* JEAN *empties her purse on to the kitchen table.*

JEAN: This is all I have left in the world. I gave everything else I had to poor Mrs Jose.
    (JIMMY *sorts through the loose change and crumpled bills.*)
    They're taking our house, everything! I can't reach your father. He's ruined.
    (*They all start to shout at once.*)
JIMMY: Is that it? Eighty-five dollars and thirty-eight cents?
DAPHNE: But we're rich. How can this happen to us?
CHLOE: (*To* TOM) Do you understand?
TOM: Yes, I do. Perfectly.
JIMMY: Well, then, explain it to me.
TOM: It's like this. A raider bought stock in your father's company, trying to buy it out. But your father outbid him, pushing the stock up. When the raider saw he couldn't take

52

over, he sold all his stock, taking a big profit, as did others, myself included. (*He is caught up in his story. Proud of his coup, he is unaware of the effect he is having, the stony looks on their faces.*) That left your father holding a lot of stock at an inflated price. Then came the story in the *Wall Street Journal* about this house holding up development and it started a stampede of selling. (*Sensing the icy atmosphere at last,* TOM *falters and stumbles to a conclusion.*) And I guess the bank stepped in and took over your father's stock and all his assets.

JEAN: (*Wailing*) Yes, they collected all the collateral. Oh, my beautiful house in Connecticut.

INT. STEWART'S OFFICE. DAY
HARRY, *the lawyer, sits head in hands, moaning.*
HARRY: It's my fault. The whole thing, going public. It's my fault.
(HAMILTON *is acutely uncomfortable.* STEWART *has a dangerous look in his eyes. He throws a bunch of computer discs across the room like frisbees.*)
STEWART: It's all yours, Hamilton. Twelve floppy discs: a life's work.

(His voice is raised and faces stare anxiously through the glass partition which gives on to the big general office. HAMILTON *glances around nervously.)*

HAMILTON: The bank would appreciate it if you'd go on running the business until we liquidate or sell or whatever we have to do.

STEWART: I'm not cut out to work for a bank. *(He pulls on his jacket, takes out his wallet and opens it out with a violent flick, revealing a chain of credit cards, driver's licence, etc. He feeds it into the mouth of a shredder. He starts to go.)*

HARRY: *(Rushing towards the shredder)* What are you doing?

HAMILTON: Stewart, where are you going?

STEWART: Out! I'm down and I'm going out. Down and out.

INT. OUTER OFFICE. DAY

He strides out into the general office. They follow him. The girls freeze at their computers, just like the illuminated photo display that lines one wall, buildings caught in the instant of collapse.

STEWART *stops and regards his staff, suddenly calm.*

STEWART: All the chains have fallen away. Desk chains, job chains. Free. I go naked into the world. I leave you everything. The debts. The doubts. The despair.

HARRY: Please don't go!

(He kisses his SECRETARY, *who is weeping softly.)*

STEWART: If I didn't screw you, I meant to. *(Turning to* HARRY*)* Your loyalty was an accusation. Blame someone else. *(A wave to the masses)* Look after yourselves, I can't any more. *(And he is gone.* HARRY *turns on the dumbstruck office workers.)*

HARRY: What are you standing around for? Get back to work!

INT. KITCHEN. DAY

JEAN *is wailing.* JIMMY *slams down the phone. He turns to the others, panic-stricken.*

JIMMY: He's gone. Walked out. Right. OK. I'm the head of the family. It's a crisis. It's OK. I'll think of something . . . I can't think of anything.

TOM: I'm ready to help out.

CHLOE: We'll manage, and without you, Tom Hudson. You

54

betrayed the whole family. I hope I never see you again.

TOM: (*Dignified*) Right. You wait. You'll come crawling. (*He gets up and heads for the door.*)

CHLOE: I will not.

DAPHNE: I might, Tom.

(TOM *goes out.*)

JIMMY: What are you saying, Chloe? We're broke. Only the rich can afford principles.

(TOM *comes back in. His proud look has collapsed into petulance.*)

TOM: This is so unfair. I was just moving money around. That's what I do. (*He turns on his heel and storms out.*)

SHERYL: Well, I guess you'll all have to look for jobs.

(*They stare at her open-mouthed. In the deathly silence they hear the anguished cries of* THE SHIT. DAPHNE, CHLOE *and* JIMMY *run out of the kitchen.*

LIONEL *and* OLIVIA *come over to* JEAN *to comfort her.*)

INT. LANDING. DAY
They run up the stairs to find THE SHIT *submerged and chained in the tank. He is crouched in it, weighted down by the chains. He survives only by forcing his body up so that his face breaks the surface for long enough to grab a mouthful of air before sinking back again.*
THE SHIT: Help! . . . Whores!
  (*They lift him out and lay him on the floor.*)
DAPHNE: Where's the key, Shitty?
THE SHIT: I swallowed it.
JIMMY: Swallowed the key? Well, let's hope it opens your
  bowels.

EXT. RIVERSIDE BY BROOKLYN BRIDGE. EVENING
STEWART *weaves from side to side as he walks. He passes down-and-outs sleeping rough. He takes an occasional swig from a bottle in a brown-paper bag. He sings softly to himself: 'Blue Moon', perhaps. He stops and stares down at the river as though seeing it for the first time. The tide is out, marooning garbage on the mud.*
STEWART: You started out as a little stream of pure water,
  trickling over rocks. How did you come to this? All mud and
  filth and little turds.

INT. UNDER AN ARCH OF BROOKLYN BRIDGE. EVENING
STEWART *reaches the line of boxes where* DAPHNE *and* THE SHIT *first met. He paces up and down, peering into the boxes, which are mostly occupied. He shouts drunkenly in at them but is ignored.*
STEWART: I'm a vagrant. Starting out. New to it. Is there a man
  among you to give advice?
  (*A black man,* MARVIN X, *comes out of his box. A dusty, frayed, three-piece suit gives him an air of faded dignity. He weighs up* STEWART *with a shrewd eye.*)
MARVIN X: These boxes are highly prized. You can't just walk in
  here with a skinful of whisky and demand one. You have to
  be talking serious money.
STEWART: (*With a dismissive wave of his arm*) Capitalist bastards
  . . . I'm finished with them.

EXT. SCRAP-METAL YARD. NIGHT
STEWART *staggers through the piles of scrap metal that abut the line of*

56

boxes. Finding a pile of old tyres he curls up on them, shifting about to find a comfortable position. They unbalance and tip over, depositing him unceremoniously into a pit of oil sludge.

INT. UNDER AN ARCH OF BROOKLYN BRIDGE. NIGHT
STEWART *crawls, covered in mud and slime, like a creature from the deep, into a vacant box.* MARVIN X *looks him over and prods him with a stick.* STEWART *kicks out a foot and snarls.*
MARVIN X: Behave yourself. You want a box? It'll cost you five.
STEWART: Three.
MARVIN X: (*Booming*) I said five.
STEWART: OK, OK, five.

INT. LIVING-ROOM. DUTCH HOUSE. NIGHT
HAMILTON *stands ill at ease in the living-room. All the members of the household are present.* THE SHIT *is slowly being freed of his chains by* JIMMY *and* DAPHNE, *who are filing away at the links with a metal saw.* CHLOE *is massaging his arm.*
HAMILTON: Without Stewart all we can do is fire the employees
    and sell off the assets, which include this house, I'm afraid.
DAPHNE: We refuse to leave.
HAMILTON: There's an eviction order ready to be served.

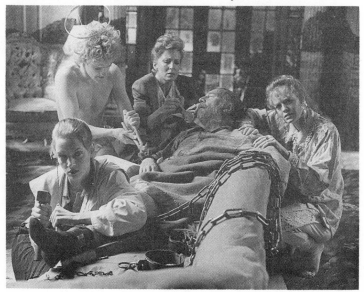

JEAN: I'm so worried about your father. Walking out like that. It's his pride. Humiliation doesn't bother me, but he's not accustomed to it.

CHLOE: Did he say where he was going?

HAMILTON: 'Down and out, and free of his chains', and that's a quote.

JIMMY: We gotta find him, take care of him.

(THE SHIT *is freed and stretches his body.*)

THE SHIT: No money. No home. He has joined the ranks of the lost and the forgotten. They will soon know the whereabouts of a new recruit.

EXT. GARBAGE DUMP. DAY

Gulls swarm over a mountain of refuse, as bulldozers pile up the garbage ever higher. Stooping men, faces masked with pieces of cloth against the foul dust, scavenge among the detritus.

STEWART *and* MARVIN X *trudge among them.* STEWART *stops. He lets out a wailing groan.* MARVIN X *consoles him.*

MARVIN X: Hey man, loosen up. You got culture shock, that's all.

(MARVIN X *gives a whoop as he retrieves a tangled coil of copper wire. He hands it to* STEWART, *who takes it absently. Two men*

fight over a kitchen chair, tumbling into the rubbish and rolling down the slope.)

STEWART: My life is over. I see that now. I'm on the scrap heap. I *am* on a scrap heap.

MARVIN X: You done big things. A lot of great men die young. They do their thing quick and get out of here.

EXT. UNDER THE ARCH. BROOKLYN BRIDGE. DAY

THE SHIT *is consulting his former neighbours.* JEAN *is kneeling down to peer into Stewart's box. She is watched by* JIMMY, CHLOE *and* DAPHNE. *She appeals to them, her voice trembling.*

JEAN: How can he live in this box? He always insists on a king-size bed.

(THE SHIT *joins them.*)

THE SHIT: He's hooked up with Marvin X. I know his haunts.

(*He heads away from the boxes, followed by the family.*)

He scavenges the dumps, he begs at the Roseland. He favours a soup kitchen on the Lower East Side.

JIMMY: We'll split up.

EXT./INT. ROSELAND BALLROOM. DAY
As JEAN *and* THE SHIT *approach, they see two bums begging at the
ballroom entrance. As the bums enter Roseland,* JEAN *and* THE SHIT
run after them, thinking that they are STEWART *and* MARVIN X. *As
they approach the bums they realize that they are not* STEWART *and*
MARVIN X. *Disappointed,* JEAN *slumps on the display of Roseland's
Hall of Fame. As she glances up at the photographs, she recognizes*
THE SHIT. *She looks over in astonishment to* THE SHIT, *who is being
welcomed with respect by the doorman of Roseland. She catches The
Shit's eye and looks back at the photograph. He gives a Maurice
Chevalier shrug. The music drifts up from the ballroom.*
THE SHIT: Shall we . . . a quickie?

INT. DANCE FLOOR. ROSELAND. DAY
A number of geriatric and arthritic couples perform intricate dance steps.
JEAN: It's been years. I've forgotten the steps.
THE SHIT: Your head has. Your heart hasn't.

EXT. GARBAGE TIP. DAY
A swell in the music from the Roseland plays as DAPHNE *and* CHLOE
*pick their way over the refuse, handkerchiefs held to their faces,
searching for their father. The gulls dip and rise. The down-and-outs
look up from their scavenging at the two pretty girls. One huge fellow
wears a balacava with just two eye-holes. He is drinking from a bottle,
sucking the beer through the knitted wool, which is wet with froth. They
are fascinated, but frightened too.*

INT. ROSELAND. DAY
A swell in the music. THE SHIT *takes* JEAN *into an ambitious spin.
They stagger, then recover. She smiles radiantly.*

INT. CHAPEL. DAY
An evangelical prayer meeting. SHERYL, *wearing earphones, sits at a
recorder.* MARCUS, *the black paranormal, assists her, holding a
microphone out to the congregation. He turns the mike to a hugely fat
woman who is speaking in tongues, babbling in some unknown
language.* THE PREACHER *anoints her with chicken blood. Ushers
scatter chicken feathers in the air. As the faithful sing out, the feathers*

ebb and flow on their breath, finally settling and sticking to the sweaty faces.

THE PREACHER: She's saying: 'God needs your dollars and he needs them now!'

(*Looking over the Preacher's shoulder,* MARCUS *sees* STEWART *and* MARVIN X, *hovering at the side of the chapel.* MARVIN X *is eating furtively while* STEWART *watches the proceedings with a half-dazed fascination. A trestle-table bearing food runs up one side of the chapel, most of it pieces of fried chicken, presumably made from those sacrificed for the ceremony.* MARVIN X *takes chicken legs and hides them about his person. He gnaws hungrily on one of them.*

THE PREACHER: (*Noticing* STEWART *at the back*) Hey, you at the back. Yes, you with the chicken leg in your hand. Come forward. Do what I say! Speak your heart, brother, speak your heart.

STEWART: (*Walking forward*) Speak my heart? Home is where the heart is. I lost my home, like a lot of other people here, I guess. Lost my family, too. Most likely losing my mind. But I know one thing. Chicken feathers ain't the answer. No, sir. You can't fight chicken-shit corporate raiders with chicken feathers, I'm telling you.

(THE PREACHER *places his palm over Stewart's eyes and daubs some blood and feathers on his forehead.*

THE PREACHER: Brother, you're half-way to speaking in tongues, 'cause we certainly can't make sense out of what you're saying.

(MARVIN X *comes to his friend's aid.*)

MARVIN X: No, Preacher, it's just jive talk from another ghetto.

(*As* MARVIN X *starts moving him away,* STEWART *sees* SHERYL, *a vision of beauty, her hair glowing with backlight, coming towards him through the crowd. She is smiling at him, a warm beatific smile.*)

STEWART: (*Softly*) I have seen the light. An angel of the Lord.

(SHERYL *comes to him, looks into his eyes, compassionate.*)

SHERYL: Hey, Mr McBain!

THE PREACHER: He has seen the light!

(MARVIN X *is faking a trance, much the way* MARCUS *did earlier.* MARCUS *taps him on the shoulder roughly. He opens one eye.*)

MARCUS: Dad. No one's looking. You can snap out of it now.

MARVIN X: Marcus. My son.
(*They fall into each other's arms. With her arms around him,*
SHERYL *leads* STEWART *out of the church.*)
SHERYL: There, there, Mr McBain. It's the Solstice. Full Moon.
You must be a Taurus. I'll get you home.

EXT. GARBAGE TIP. DAY
DAPHNE *and* CHLOE *are fleeing, but their way is blocked by the big
man with the balaclava. As they try to pass him to the left, he steps to
the left. They go right, he goes right. It is like a dance and it matches
the beat of the dance tune on the soundtrack.*

INT. ROSELAND. DAY
The dance ends. THE SHIT *and* JEAN *are laughing and applauding,
when* JEAN *suddenly remembers* STEWART *and runs out of Roseland.*

EXT. GARBAGE TIP. DAY
The girls dart, one each side of the big man, and make their escape.

Black, fade to:

INT. LIVING-ROOM. DUTCH HOUSE. DAY
STEWART *is lying on the sofa under a blanket.* JEAN *sleeps, sitting in
an armchair at his side. He awakes and looks round the room. In his
weakened state everything appears heightened and warped.*

SHERYL *is sitting in her yoga position against one of the paintings.
The 'live paintings' on the walls lead his eye into infinite vistas of
imaginary worlds. He turns his head and glimpses* JIMMY *at the
glowing green screen of his computer. Jimmy's tapping on the keyboard
sounds, to* STEWART, *like jungle crickets.* STEWART *gets to his feet
unsteadily and staggers towards the conservatory.*

INT. CONSERVATORY. DAY
STEWART *enters the conservatory and pushes aside the foliage,
revealing an enchanted forest stretching away before him. One tree
looks almost human. He gasps and stumbles towards it. The tree
moves, turns and smiles at* STEWART. *It is* LIONEL, *dressed and
painted as a tree.*
LIONEL: You feeling yourself again, Mr McBain?
(STEWART *is startled.* CHLOE *leans past him and continues to*

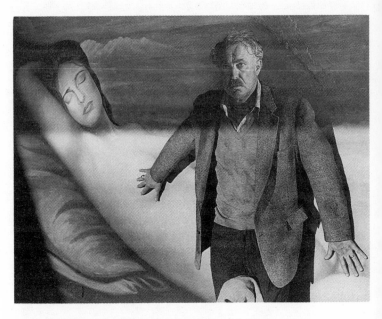

paint Lionel's body so that it merges with the forest.)

CHLOE: You definitely look better than you did yesterday. Half dead and babbling.

STEWART: Speaking in tongues, probably.

CHLOE: Aren't you ashamed of yourself?

(STEWART *looks about him confused, perplexed.*)

STEWART: All of this, all of you, sprang from my loins? My offspring?

DAPHNE: (*Voice over*) Daddy, look!

(*He turns and* DAPHNE, *in her magician's outfit, pulls a white dove from nowhere. It flies past* STEWART, *up into the foliage.* DAPHNE *speaks reproachfully.*)

I've decided to forgive you.

(*She skips away from him, to be instantly replaced by* OLIVIA. *She swirls around* STEWART *in diaphanous chiffon, seeking Lionel's approval.*)

OLIVIA: I don't think they should be cut on the bias, Lionel.

LIONEL: (*Irritably*) You wear them, I'll design them . . . (*He squints.*) Maybe you're right.

(STEWART *finds himself surrounded by laughing girls and*

*billowing silk. Suddenly a hand grabs his arm. It is Jimmy's. He
sits his father down in front of the computer and hands him a
control box.* STEWART *hesitates, looking at the screen in a
puzzled way.*)

JIMMY: Now, you have to press here and try to stop me from
demolishing your building. Come on, it's user-friendly.
(STEWART *stares dumbly at the computer screen. A title reads
'Demolish the Taj Mahal'. A wrecking ball crashes into it,
destroying the domed roof.*)
You have to try and get your little man out of the crumbling
building while I try and destroy your exits.

STEWART: But it's the Taj Mahal.

JIMMY: (*Gently*) It's only a game, Dad. Got the idea from you.
Demolition.
(*The game continues.* STEWART *desperately tries to escape but
Jimmy's ball and chain keep making dead ends. Every time they
hit the building,* STEWART *cries out. Yet another exit crumbles
before his eyes. For a moment* STEWART *himself is projected into
the game. He sees himself trapped, rubble crumbling in on him.
He cries out. A great bellow of anguish comes up from deep inside
him.* JIMMY *stops the game, alarmed.*)
I thought you'd be pleased.
(JEAN *wakes with a start and* THE SHIT *bursts into the room,
hearing* STEWART's *cries.* STEWART *strides out of the
conservatory and into the living-room. Everybody follows,
concerned.* STEWART *slumps back on to the couch, head in
hands.* JEAN *sits down next to him and puts her arm around his
shoulders.*)

JEAN: Try and rest, Stewart. It's nothing serious. Just a nervous
breakdown.

STEWART: Everything has broken down. Values, the family,
America, honest labour. Everything I ever stood for.
Gone.

JIMMY: You've got all that out of the way, Dad. You can start
living.
(STEWART *searches their faces as they form an arc around the
couch.* JIMMY *is chastened.*)
Only kidding.

STEWART: (*Wearily*) I bet there's not a single cause that any one of
you would stand up and fight for? Is there?

(*They look sheepishly at each other and 'um' and 'er'.*)

DAPHNE: Well, there's the bald eagle, but I wouldn't fight for it. I'm a pacifist.

(LIONEL *struggles to contribute.* THE SHIT *hopes his mumbles will pass as a positive contribution.*)

CHLOE: I'm sure there's something. I just can't think of it right now.

DAPHNE: (*Shaking her head*) I suppose deep down we're shallow.

(STEWART *is nodding off. They all tiptoe out of the room and into the hallway, leaving* JEAN *to watch over* STEWART. *She peers down at her unshaven, wild-looking husband.*)

JEAN: I can read you like a book and you're still a stranger.

INT. HALLWAY. DAY

The doorbell rings. DAPHNE *opens it. A tall* MAN *is smiling warmly.*

MAN: McBain.

EVERYBODY: Yes.

(*He steps inside and quickly touches each one of them with a document he holds in his hand and gives it to* JIMMY.)

MAN: Writ for eviction duly served. Good morning. Thank you.

(*He leaves.* DAPHNE *slams the door and throws her body against it.*)

DAPHNE: I'm not budging and that's that.

(JIMMY *drops the order as though it were contaminated.*)

LIONEL: We can't leave. I show the collection in a week and then we'll all be rich.

(DAPHNE *stamps her foot on the eviction order.*)

JIMMY: Even if we do hang in here, we're still broke.

CHLOE: Maybe I could get the insurance company to give me an advance for the calendar.

JIMMY: I'd better go find Tom.

CHLOE: We don't need charity from that traitor.

THE SHIT, LIONEL and DAPHNE: Oh yes, we do.

INT. LOBBY. INSURANCE COMPANY. DAY

CHLOE *is suitably intimidated by the soaring atrium and the busy foyer, which presumably was the architect's intention. She hovers by the reception desk, listening to the clickclack of expensive shoe leather on the marble floor. Lionel's father,* JOHN, *greets her.*

JOHN: Chloe! Welcome! Sorry to hear about your father's problems. (*He makes a sweeping gesture, to include the lobby area.*) Try to imagine it. Huge blow-ups of your calendar right here in the lobby.

(*They thread their way through trees to get to the lift.*)

CHLOE: They're cutting down all the forests and planting the trees indoors instead.

(JOHN *gives her an odd look.*)

Anyway, that's what my sister says.

(*He leads her into the lift. He frowns and drops his voice.*)

JOHN: How's my son, Lionel?

CHLOE: Making some lovely dresses.

JOHN: Not wearing them, I hope.

(*The lift doors close, concealing* CHLOE's *response.*)

INT. STOCKBROKER'S OFFICE. DAY

JIMMY *makes his way through rows of frenzied dealers. They scream, they shout, they make frantic signals across the floor.* JIMMY, *quite indifferent to the mayhem, reaches Tom's desk but finds it vacant. He approaches Tom's two neighbours and tries to catch their attention.*

JIMMY: Tom Hudson. Where is he?

(They completely ignore him. The first dealer is weeping as he sits hunched over his phone. EDGAR *is on his feet yelling across at another dealer and then screaming numbers into a phone.* JIMMY *shouts into Edgar's face.)*

JIMMY: Tom! Where's Tom?

(He gets no response. He glances at Edgar's phone number, sits on Tom's desk and taps it out. EDGAR *grabs the phone on the first ring, holding it to his spare ear.)*

JIMMY: Where the fuck is Tom?

*(EDGAR *gives not a glance at* JIMMY, *who is only three feet away from him.)*

EDGAR: Tom's gone down to the floor, trying to salvage something from the shipwreck.

*(JIMMY *puts the phone down and turns to* EDGAR, *their faces inches apart.)*

JIMMY: Sorry to hang up on you.

*(EDGAR *spares him only a puzzled glance.)*

INT. CONFERENCE ROOM. INSURANCE COMPANY. DAY
A high cavern of a room with girders spidering the walls and ceiling. Chloe's calendar pictures flash on to a large screen. Some of the insurance company's senior executives watch from a sprawl of couches

and armchairs. Lionel's father, JOHN, *representing the advertising agency, smiles encouragingly, urging her on.* CHLOE *is a tiny figure next to the screen, embarrassed and giving a feeble commentary.*

CHLOE: February, broken hearts . . . April, water damage . . . November, pestilence, plague and stuff . . . December, broken windows . . . May is, well . . . July, could be . . .
> (JOHN *jumps in, covering for her.*)

JOHN: Absolutely brilliant. It's the environment. It's nature. It's *us*. And I love the clever suggestion of lurking disaster – fire, earthquake, flood. Remember, you guys have a first here. (*He points at an imaginary banner above him.*) 'Acts of God. Only we insure against them.'

CHLOE: (*Blurting out*) I really need an advance to finish the sequence. I know payment is on delivery, but if you could possibly . . .

JOHN: I don't see that as an insuperable problem. Do you, Oshima-san?
> (MR OSHIMA, *the senior executive, is listening intently to his secretary, who has come nervously into the room and is talking urgently into his ear. He rises to his feet and manages a few strangled words before dashing out of the door, passing in front of the screen.*)

OSHIMA: The market has crashed!
> (*The executives all rise to follow him, including* JOHN. *Enraged,* CHLOE *catches* JOHN *by the arm. The slides keep on changing, making an ironic commentary on their confrontation.*)

CHLOE: Oh no you don't! I've grovelled. I've compromised my art. We're broke. We're being evicted. Your own son is starving.

JOHN: As you can see, we all have our problems. Finish the sequence. You have a contract. They'll have to pay.
> (*He struggles to escape her grasp. She hangs on.*)
> For Chrissake let me go. I'm in the market too. I'm probably getting killed out there.

CHLOE: You might get killed in here.
> (*He breaks loose.* CHLOE *falls back into the screen, crashing into one of her own landscapes.*)

INT. STOCK-MARKET FLOOR. DAY
It is naked panic and raging hysteria. The dealers on the floor stand under the big board. They fight and clamour and send back tic-tac

67

signals to their partners at the desks, who are in telephone contact with clients, banks, insurance companies and stockbrokers.

JIMMY *struggles through the mob, searching for* TOM. *He finally spots him curled up on the floor in a foetal position. His eyes are glazed.* JIMMY *shakes him.*

JIMMY: You been sniffing something? Listen. Come home. All is forgiven. We need your money and you need us.

TOM: The bottom's dropped out of the market. I'm wiped out. I'd slit my wrists if I could afford a razor. And you're looking to borrow money from me?

(TOM *laughs, a disturbing, hysterical laugh.* JIMMY *slaps his face.*)

What did you do that for?

JIMMY: Hysteria. You did it to my mother.

(TOM *punches Jimmy's arm. They start to wrestle on the floor, giggling. Suddenly a* TV *cameraman and lights are focused on them. A woman* REPORTER *narrates into her mike, shouting over the din.*)

REPORTER: . . . and as the stock market continues in turmoil, fights are breaking out between dealers . . . is this the end of capitalism as we know it?

(JIMMY *and* TOM *stop and sit up, blinking at the lights.*)

INT. BATHROOM. DUTCH HOUSE. DAY

STEWART *stands before the bathroom mirror. He has a three-day growth of beard. He stares long and hard at his reflection.*

STEWART: I don't know who you are, but I'm going to shave you anyway.

INT. LIVING-ROOM. DAY

THE SHIT, *wearing a long robe, with an entranced look on his face, has one arm outstretched. The other hand is resting on Daphne's head. She is sitting upright in a chair.*

SHERYL *watches them, fascinated.*

DAPHNE: (*Medium-like*) You see, Sheryl, you find it easier to talk to paranormals than to normals. That's because real people aren't real for you. You can't relate because you've got no relations.

SHERYL: Oh God, you've seen right through me.

(THE SHIT *looks at* DAPHNE *nervously, then addresses* SHERYL.)

THE SHIT: I taught her how to fake it, but it turns out she has a
genuine gift . . . And then, as a finale, I plan to do a little
levitation.
(*He leans back and his legs rise into the air until his whole body is
horizontal.*)
SHERYL: I knew it. Everything is possible in this house!
Wait a minute . . .
(THE SHIT *lifts his long gown to reveal that he is holding out a
pair of artificial legs horizontally, while his own are planted
firmly on the floor. He smirks.* SHERYL *grins and groans at her
own gullibility.*)
Almost anything.

INT. HALLWAY. DAY
JEAN *appears from the kitchen, whipping eggs, as* STEWART *descends
the stairs.*
JEAN: I've never seen you looking so calm, Stewart.
STEWART: Beaten would be a better word.
JEAN: Oh, don't say that.
STEWART: (*Smiling*) Couldn't even make it as a bum.
(*He passes her and goes to the hall mirror to adjust his tie.*)
JEAN: Why are you smiling? No guilty feelings? No sense of
shame? Remorse?
STEWART: (*Calm*) You can't provoke me, Jean. All the anger's
gone too.
JEAN: Well, what are you going to do?
STEWART: Whatever I'm told.
JEAN: You? Do what you're told?
STEWART: I kicked them out, they took me in. I'll do what I'm
told.
(JEAN *looks sceptical.*

The two INDIAN WOMEN *come down the stairs clutching bags
and coats.* LIONEL *follows them down the stairs, pleading with
them.*)
LIONEL: Purna, Mya, please!
(*They shake their heads firmly.*)
PURNA: No pay. No way.
LIONEL: Just give me a week, for the sake of Allah or whomever.
(*As the women leave the house they pass* JIMMY, *supporting a*

catatonic TOM, *entering through the front door.* LIONEL, *still pleading, runs after them.*

JEAN *comes face to face with her son and* TOM, *who is groaning.*)
JIMMY: Stock market crashed again. Tom's in shock.
(CHLOE *comes stumbling in behind them, carrying a carousel of slides and her portfolio.*)
CHLOE: (*Lip quivering*) So am I. They wouldn't pay.
(STEWART *twitches at the sight of* TOM, *but holds himself in control.* TOM *comes to himself, grunts irritably and looks spitefully at his companions. It is all too much for* CHLOE. *She falls into her mother's arms, sobbing.*)

INT. LIVING-ROOM. DAY
SHERYL *is sobbing while* THE SHIT *swings a watch chain before her eyes.*
SHERYL: My parents divorced when I was nine. Families confuse me.
DAPHNE: They confuse me too.
THE SHIT: . . . four and five and six . . .
SHERYL: You're so right. I just can't handle relationships. (*She is overcome by sobbing and crying.*)
THE SHIT: (*Consoling*) Think of a wheat field swaying in the wind . . .
(*Shouts and screams from the hallway distract them.* SHERYL *and* THE SHIT *start for the door in alarm, but* DAPHNE *does not stir. She is in a trance, hypnotized.* THE SHIT *hesitates, throws her a worried look, then dashes out.*)

INT. HALLWAY. DAY
STEWART *takes a deep breath, trying to control his rising anger, then lunges for* TOM, *colliding with* LIONEL, *who has returned, head in hands.* STEWART *throws him aside and grabs* TOM *by the lapels, driving him back towards the door.*
STEWART: Out of my house, Judas!
(TOM *has* JIMMY *and* CHLOE *on each arm and together they push* STEWART *back again.* SHERYL *and* THE SHIT *appear and try to pull them apart.*)
TOM: Your house? It's more my house than it is your house with all the useless shares I have in American Demolition.

71

(*Stewart's rage gives him strength. He drives them back again.*)

STEWART: You little swine. You ruined me!

TOM: I tried to save you and it ruined me!

(*They stop, panting for breath, eyeball to eyeball.*)

STEWART: Save *me*? Save *me*?

TOM: I thought your stock had hit bottom. I spent every last dollar I had to buy it up to keep the business in the family. Now, with the crash, it's worthless.

JEAN: I don't understand, but I'm very touched.

(THE SHIT *dashes back into the living-room.*)

INT. LIVING-ROOM. DAY

THE SHIT *clicks his fingers in front of Daphne's glazed eyes.*

THE SHIT: Snap out of it. You know I can't hypnotize to save my life.

(*She snaps out of it, gets up and walks straight out into the hallway, much to relief of* THE SHIT.)

INT. HALLWAY. DAY

LIONEL *is sitting on the stairs, banging his head against the wall in despair.* JEAN *is in a chair holding* CHLOE *in her arms.* STEWART *is slumped over the banister. The others lean against the walls, panting, or slide to their knees, whimpering with despair.* SHERYL *is still sobbing.* JIMMY *comforts her.*

DAPHNE: (*Still bemused*) I feel great. Isn't life wonderful?

STEWART: Yes, it is. I don't have to do anything.

DAPHNE: But let's do *something*.

    (*The others stare at* DAPHNE *in astonishment.* JEAN *perks up.*)

JEAN: Lionel, if we all pitched in, couldn't you still get the show ready in time?

    (SHERYL *looks up through her tears.*)

SHERYL: I can sew.

JIMMY: So what? So can I.

SHERYL: What?

JIMMY: (*Laughing*) Sew.

    (LIONEL *gets up, touched.*)

LIONEL: Would you? You'd do that for me?

DAPHNE: We'll sew our hearts out!

LIONEL: What about Chloe's calendar?

CHLOE: I'll finish that too.

    (*They are suddenly light-hearted.*)

THE SHIT: (*Sarcastic*) Let's do the show right here in the barn.

TOM: (*Hopefully*) Can I be a part of this? I'll pitch in.

    (CHLOE *smiles at* TOM. *He is forgiven.*

    They all follow LIONEL *up the stairs, leaving* STEWART *stranded below.*)

STEWART: Just tell me what to do. I'll do it.

INT. LIONEL'S WORKROOM. DAY

They all work feverishly, sewing, cutting, fitting. LIONEL *works on* OLIVIA, *tucking and pinning.* SHERYL *and* JIMMY *sit at the sewing machines.* JIMMY *looks over at* SHERYL, *distracted. His tie gets caught in the machine.* DAPHNE *is cutting a pattern.* TOM *is cleaning the floor around her. Their eyes meet, briefly.* THE SHIT *is at the ironing board.* STEWART *is sewing a beaded collar, spectacles on his nose.* LIONEL *supervises the work, the master of all he surveys. Intercut with these workroom activities is:*

73

INT. LIVING-ROOM. DAY
A huge canvas painted with Van Gogh waves. CHLOE *paints*
STEWART'*s body so that it appears to be submerged in the ocean. She*
then paints SHERYL, DAPHNE *and herself so that they become waves.*
Painting her father's face brings them into an intense intimacy.
CHLOE: . . . I clung to your neck and you swam miles out to sea.
    And I wasn't afraid because you were the strongest daddy in
    the world.
STEWART: I thought I would live for ever and, now you've grown
    and gone, I'm clinging to the wreckage.
CHLOE: Then this wave hit us and swept me away from you. And
    even as I was drowning I still trusted you. And when you
    finally plucked me out of the sea, I saw the fear on your face
    and *then* I was afraid.
STEWART: Me too. (*Smiles, deeply moved.*)

    (*Later.* JIMMY *is behind the camera.* CHLOE *arranges the two*
    girls and then herself so that they perfectly match the backing.
    Chloe's arm reaches and holds Stewart's outstretched hand,
    saving him from drowning. CHLOE, *seeing Stewart's expression,*
    perplexed and pained, calls out:)
CHLOE: Now, Jimmy, now.

(JIMMY *clicks away.*)

JIMMY: That's the last of the film.

CHLOE: Eleven months out of twelve. Just one more to do and all
that money waiting for us.

INT. LIONEL'S WORKROOM. DAY

The collection is finished and hangs on the racks. DAPHNE, CHLOE,
OLIVIA, JEAN *and* SHERYL *lie squashed and exhausted on Lionel's
bed.* TOM *and* JIMMY *lie at their feet.* STEWART *is at the cutting table,
head in hands.* THE SHIT *is stretched out on the cutting table,
exhausted.* LIONEL *paces the room.*

DAPHNE: (*Doubtfully*) Well, at least we finished it.

CHLOE: *We* know it's beautiful.

LIONEL: But I want the world to know it's beautiful. If we could
just afford the venue and the models to show it . . .

THE SHIT: So near yet so far.

STEWART: (*From his sleep*) Hell. If we all got jobs for a couple of
weeks we could put the money together.

INT. UNEMPLOYMENT BUREAU. DAY

There are several cubicles and each has a line of people waiting.
STEWART *has reached the head of his.* CHLOE *is behind him with* TOM.

STEWART: Bulldozers.

CLERK: (*Patronizingly*) Not at your age.

(STEWART *leans forward menacingly.*)

STEWART: I have a high-explosives licence and a vengeful nature.

(*In the next line it is Jean's turn.* DAPHNE, SHERYL *and* JIMMY
wait behind her.)

JEAN: Experience? Well, I'm a buyer.

CLERK: Which stores have you bought for?

JEAN: Most of them. From them, not for them.

(DAPHNE *elbows past her mother.*)

DAPHNE: Daphne McBain, magician's assistant. Fortune telling,
ESP.

CLERK: You read minds? Then I don't have to tell you what
vacancies I got, do I?

DAPHNE: No you don't. (*She turns away.*)

EXT. DUTCH HOUSE. DAY

CHLOE, DAPHNE, JEAN, STEWART, THE SHIT, LIONEL, JIMMY,

SHERYL *and* TOM *return home from the Unemployment Bureau.*

THE SHIT *and* JIMMY *start running towards the house.* JIMMY *skips from stone to stone agilely.* THE SHIT *runs through the wet mud. Two men are sealing the windows and doors. A pile of belongings stands just outside the house.*

JIMMY: (*Grabbing one man*) What is this?

MAN: Eviction . . .

JIMMY: This is America. Don't we have rights?

MAN: Not without money you don't.

(TOM *arrives on the scene, pulling* JIMMY *away.*)

TOM: There's obviously been a computer error here.

JIMMY: Don't blame the computer for this.

(THE SHIT *runs up and grabs the other man, who throws him into the mud.*)

THE SHIT: (*Sitting in the mud*) Jesus, a man can't even ask a question.

(*The others come rushing up.* JEAN *and* DAPHNE *go over to* THE SHIT, *who makes no attempt to get up.*)

I slipped. Compulsory eight count.

DAPHNE: You were very brave.

JEAN: This is more than I can stand. The third house I've lost in a week.

(DAPHNE *and* JEAN *help* THE SHIT *up and carry him over to a chair.* JIMMY *has climbed up the house and is trying to pry away the wood that has been nailed to the windows.* TOM *and* STEWART *are with the eviction man.*)

MAN: You've been evicted. Accept it.

(*The man walks away.* TOM *follows.*)

STEWART: (*Calmly*) I can accept it.

(*He explodes*) Bastard!

(STEWART *turns towards the house, takes a run at the door and charges it with his shoulder. It doesn't budge. He lets out a cry and clutches his shoulder.* SHERYL *comes over and kneels down by a puddle.*)

SHERYL: Oh, my Tarot cards!

(LIONEL *is sorting through the pile of belongings, checking his material and dresses.*)

LIONEL: It's all right, calm down. My collection is safe.

JEAN: What'll we do?

CHLOE: (*Kindly*) Why don't you stay with a friend?

JEAN: And desert you all in your hour of need? I wouldn't dream of it.

STEWART: (*Clutching his arm and through gritted teeth*) She has no friends. Only relations.

DAPHNE: Let's load up the trailer.

(*They all start to gather their things up and move towards the trailer.*)

Couldn't your parents help us, Lionel?

LIONEL: Dad was wiped out by the crash, too.

TOM: I can't believe they haven't repossessed the Porsche yet.

STEWART: I'm gonna lean on that son-of-a-bitch Hamilton. He dumped us in the street, he's obligated to take us in.

(*They start to pile things into the trailer.*)

EXT. DUTCH HOUSE. TWILIGHT

The Porsche pulls away from the house. TOM *is driving. The others, with all their possessions, are in the trailer. The house is left, abandoned in the desolate landscape.*

EXT. TOP OF TRAILER. EVENING
The group are now sitting on the top of their belongings, like the family in The Grapes of Wrath. *The trailer is attached to the Porsche and is pulled through the Manhattan streets. Stewart's arm is bound up in a flowered silk scarf.*

EXT. HAMILTON'S HOUSE. MANHATTAN. NIGHT
The Porsche and the trailer pull up outside Hamilton's house. As STEWART *climbs down from the trailer and strides up to the front door,* HAMILTON *emerges, holding a suitcase.*
STEWART: Hamilton, where do you think you're going?
HAMILTON: Margot's thrown me out of the house.
STEWART: Why?
HAMILTON: The bank fired me for backing lunatic schemes like yours. The computer identified me as ineffective.
STEWART: Jesus, Hamilton. You better come with us.
(STEWART *takes Hamilton's suitcase and tosses it on to the trailer with his good arm. The others watch, perplexed.*)

EXT. MANHATTAN STREETS. NIGHT
It is raining. The Porsche and trailer approach a shabby building. It is a Welfare Shelter. The members of the group have improvised protection from the rain, wrapping themselves in odd bits of plastic.
DAPHNE: They better give us rooms. We pay taxes for these places.
STEWART: You pay taxes? *I* pay taxes! They owe *me*!
THE SHIT: No way do I set foot in there. Why do you think every self-respecting down-and-out sleeps in the street? Because he doesn't relish the idea of being robbed, knifed and raped in a Welfare Shelter.
(*As they pull up at the kerb, they see an unsavoury collection of derelicts, drug addicts and bag ladies hanging around outside. Heavy rain now falls.* TOM *gets out of the car.*)
STEWART: (*To* TOM) Haul ass!
TOM: Where to?
STEWART: The bridge.
TOM: What?
STEWART: The Brooklyn Bridge.

EXT. TRAILER. MANHATTAN STREETS. NIGHT
They are driving through the wet streets. The family group is visible only through a sheet of plastic that now covers the trailer. Rain runs over it, distorting the distressed faces peering through.

EXT. BROOKLYN BRIDGE. NIGHT
Under the arches a group of tramps, including MARVIN X, *armed with sticks and batons, defend their ground against* LIONEL, THE SHIT, JIMMY, TOM STEWART, DAPHNE, CHLOE *and* JEAN.

MARVIN X: (*Menacingly*) OK, Stewart has a box, but not the rest of you. We are a well-established down-and-out community. We cannot be overrun by penniless fly-by-nights.
(MARCUS *emerges from one of the boxes, stretching sleepily. He is startled to see his friends.*)

MARCUS: It's OK, Dad, they're my friends.

MARVIN X: (*Turning angrily on his son*) You get back in your box and keep out of this.
(*The penniless fly-by-nights back away, then turn to the Porsche. They have nowhere to go. They huddle together. The rain lashes against their faces.*)

THE SHIT: This is as low as you can get. This is whale shit. The bottom of the ocean. (*To Daphne*) I was better off in my box!

JEAN: (*Brightly*) Well, as least now there is nowhere to go but up.
(*They glower at her.*)

SHERYL: I guess I'll take a plane back home to LA.

JIMMY: LA? We've sunk that low?

TOM: Home to step-mother.

DAPHNE: What?

TOM: Humiliation before hunger.
(MARCUS *appears at Sheryl's side. He looks at her sheepishly.*)

MARCUS: Dad's thrown me out of the house.
(*The group embraces sadly and shakes hands, the tight bonds that bound them falling away. Thunder and lightning rack the sky.* STEWART *shakes his fists at the heavens.*)

STEWART: Rain's not enough, huh? A tempest now!

JIMMY: (*Lighting up*) Dad, there might be a way. The Dutch House. It's structurally unstable, right?

STEWART: Well, so what?

JIMMY: Do you think a storm like this could . . . ?

TOM: (*Snapping his fingers*) Knock it down? Got it.

JIMMY: With a little help. Dad, do you still have the keys to the explosives store?

EXT. DUTCH HOUSE. NIGHT
The house, its windows boarded up, is whipped by rain and wind. A hundred yards away, the Porsche and trailer are parked. A piece of transparent plastic sheeting covers the trailer. Under it, the forms of JEAN, DAPHNE, CHLOE, SHERYL, THE SHIT, MARCUS *and* LIONEL *can be seen. They peer out through the rip in the plastic.*

INT. PORSCHE AND TRAILER. NIGHT
STEWART *and* TOM *sit in the front seat.* JIMMY *and* HAMILTON *are crushed into the back, their heads thrust forward between the other two.* STEWART *holds a remote-control detonator. He looks distracted. They watch him anxiously.*
JIMMY: (*Nervous*) We're gonna pull it off. I feel it. I know it.
TOM: No one will notice the explosions with all this thunder.
STEWART: Now it comes to it, I haven't got the stomach for it any more.
JIMMY: Dad, you're a pro. Just one last shot.
STEWART: I don't know, son.
JIMMY: Dad, look at us!
    (*Watching the house from the slit in the plastic sheeting,* JEAN *turns to* CHLOE.)
DAPHNE: I loved that house.
THE SHIT: You hated it.
JEAN: Your lovely paintings.
CHLOE: They're just backgrounds. What matters is on film.
    (*In the Porsche* STEWART *still hesitates.*)
HAMILTON: Stewart, it solves everything. With the house gone, the site can be sold. The bank paid off. I'll be exonerated.
STEWART: What about the country house?
HAMILTON: Jean will get her house back.
STEWART: Anything due to me, I want split between Harry and the workers.
TOM: Mine will go to the family.
STEWART: Your family?
TOM: Your family.
    (STEWART *is touched. His mind is made up. He taps the detonator, pauses and taps it again. A rumbling sequence of explosions.*)

80

EXT. DUTCH HOUSE. NIGHT
Miniature. The roof of the house lifts up and flies off.

INT. PORSCHE. NIGHT
STEWART *taps out another sequence on the detonator.*

EXT. DUTCH HOUSE. NIGHT
*Miniature. The front of the house cracks, crumbles and seems to be
blown away by the storm. Passers-by watch in amazement. A cop
reaches for his walkie-talkie. He shakes his head in amazement,
clearly convinced that the storm is doing the damage. Another wall
appears to crash before the storm. Under the plastic sheet the occupants
of the trailer watch, awe-struck.*

INT. PORSCHE. NIGHT
JIMMY: That was your masterpiece, Dad.
STEWART: And my swan song.

EXT. DUTCH HOUSE. NIGHT
*A jagged wall is left standing. On it is one of Chloe's paintings: a view
of an idyllic landscape. Rain beats down on it.*

EXT. COUNTRY HOUSE. DAY
*A landscape not unlike the one painted on the wall of the Dutch
House.*

CHLOE *is reconstructing Manet's painting* Déjeuner sur l'Herbe.
STEWART *and* JIMMY *are the two men, dressed in period costume.*
SHERYL *is discreetly naked and looks directly at camera. Beyond is*
DAPHNE, *the second girl, paddling in the lake behind the picnickers.
In the foreground are the discarded clothes and picnic remains. They
all keep perfectly still and for a moment it appears to be a painting.*
CHLOE *comparing it with the reproduction that stands on an easel
beside her, lines up the shot through her camera.*
CHLOE: It has to do with the sadness that all things pass away and
    how Manet captured one of those rare perfect moments in
    life.
STEWART: (*Studying the painting*) I guess it was. (*He looks at the
    others, smiling.*)
    I guess this is too, eh, Jimmy?

JIMMY: It was. As soon as you say it, it isn't.
STEWART: (*Getting up*) Can I take these clothes off now?
SHERYL: Can I put mine on?
CHLOE: That concludes the calendar, folks.
    (JIMMY *pulls a towel out from behind him and drapes it over*
    SHERYL's *nakedness*.)
JIMMY: (*Whispers in her ear*) You've got a perfect pair of . . .

(SHERYL *looks at him threateningly.*)

. . . I mean they're a perfect match. (*He jumps up, pulling off the clothes he wore for the painting.*)

Take me, I'm yours.

(SHERYL *hits him. He squeals towards the lake.*)

Help! Rape!

(DAPHNE *still holds her pose, standing in the lake.*)

DAPHNE: Is it over? Nobody ever tells me anything.

(*As* DAPHNE *is getting up she sprays water on* STEWART *and, blaming it on* JIMMY, *she runs away. Furious,* STEWART *challenges* JIMMY *to a game of Slap, defeating him and shoving* JIMMY *in the pond. As* STEWART *is laughing at* JIMMY'S *predicament,* DAPHNE *comes up behind him, pushes him in the water and runs off.* CHLOE *dismantles her camera from the tripod. Behind her stands a large country house with a grand flight of steps stretching down from a terrace.* TOM *and* JEAN *are walking backwards, looking up at the house. They approach* CHLOE.)

JEAN: Tom is a genius, getting the deeds back for the house.

TOM: Debts paid and enough cash to get by on . . .

CHLOE: And I thought The Shit was the greatest con-artist the world has ever known.

TOM: It's the art of business. I'm an artist too. I've worked it all

83

out with your mother. You get that wing – it's got wonderful north light. I've got lovely workrooms for Lionel, and Jimmy can set up his video-game research over there. It's supposed to be haunted. That'll keep Sheryl happy. And I can handle *our* investments with a fax and a phone in any old spare room.

CHLOE: One thing we've learned. We need a lot less than we used to.

(DAPHNE *joins them.*)

DAPHNE: And it's going to be an ecology zone, isn't it, Tom?

(TOM *takes her hands in his. They look into each other's eyes.*)

TOM: Solar heating.

DAPHNE: No aerosols.

TOM: Organic vegetables.

DAPHNE: And all spare cash to the homeless.

TOM: (*Reluctant*) Well, OK.

DAPHNE: Promise?

TOM: Promise.

(*Later, in a shady place under the trees,* STEWART *is stretched out on the grass asleep. There is the sound of music. He opens his eyes. Through a gap in the foliage he has a glimpse of ethereal creatures moving back and forth in the strange light. One of them starts towards him. As it nears, he sees it is* DAPHNE *in her conjuror's assistant's outfit. She blocks out his view for a moment but reveals it again. This time* STEWART *realizes what he has been watching is* LIONEL *rehearsing his fashion show with* THE SHIT *acting as an MC.*)

STEWART: Daphne, I just saw the light.

DAPHNE: You mean the answer, the truth?

STEWART: No. Just the light falling in a certain way.

DAPHNE: (*Sitting down on the grass beside him*) But what does it all mean? Why are we here? What's the point of life?

STEWART: The point is . . . moments like this.

DAPHNE: You mean this is it? We're not getting ready for something? We're just getting ready . . . for nothing?

STEWART: (*Looking at* LIONEL *and the models*) I think it's a rehearsal.

DAPHNE: (*Brightening*) For another life?

(STEWART *looks at her fondly and laughs.*)

STEWART: (*Stroking her hair*) For the fashion show.

84

DAPHNE: (*Amused and exasperated*) Oh, Dad.

EXT. HOUSE TERRACE AND STEPS. EVENING
Lionel's fashion show is reaching its climax. Among the audience is a group of fashion buyers, watching intently. LIONEL *searches their faces, desperate for a clue to their reaction. They are stony. The family, Lionel's father,* JOHN, HAMILTON *and* MARCUS *are also there.*

The models, SHERYL, CHLOE *and* OLIVIA *among them, are dressed in Lionel's wild and eccentric clothes for the finale. They are all pressing forward in a worked-out formation.* THE SHIT *is resplendent in top hat and tails. He is confident and commanding. Assisted by* DAPHNE, *he engineers puffs of coloured smoke from which each girl and each new costume appear.*

A shower of silver sparks and a large puff of smoke reveal LIONEL. *The buyers applaud him enthusiastically.*

Later everyone is partying and dancing under the Chinese lanterns that hang from the trees. LIONEL *is surrounded by the admiring buyers.* JIMMY *is dancing with* SHERYL. *He tries to hold her tightly in his arms, but she manages to keep him at a slight distance.* STEWART *and* DAPHNE *lean against a tree, watching.*
STEWART: Life's just a big game to that kid.

DAPHNE: But he takes his games very seriously.

STEWART: (*Teasing*) Perhaps *that's* the answer, Daphne.

(JIMMY *moves his hand up and down Sheryl's back.*)

JIMMY: I'm crazy about you, Sheryl. All I think about is you. I can't even look at another girl.

(*Over Sheryl's shoulder he catches the model Olivia's eye. She smiles at him.*)

SHERYL: Jimmy, I'm very fond of you. You're funny, you're cute, but you're so immature. I mean, if you could just grow up, maybe I could learn to . . .

(JIMMY *has wandered off into the inviting arms of* OLIVIA, *leaving* SHERYL *to finish her sentence alone.*)

JIMMY: I'm crazy about you, Olivia. All I think about is you. I can't even look at another girl.

OLIVIA: I love you too, Jimmy.

JIMMY: (*Astonished*) You do?

(CHLOE *and* TOM *dance past* STEWART *and* DAPHNE.)

STEWART: That boy's a bit of an asshole. He reminds me of myself at his age.

DAPHNE: Oh, no, I don't think he'll be like you, when he's your age. I think he'll be really nice.

(*She clamps her hand to her mouth, realizing her gaffe.*)

STEWART: (*Winces*) I'm making an effort in that direction.

(TOM *looks down into Chloe's eyes.*)

TOM: Why do you think I'm doing all this? For my own ego?

CHLOE: I know, I know, you're doing it for me. And don't think I don't appreciate it . . .

TOM: Chloe, stop. I'm doing all this . . . everything . . . for Daphne.

(TOM *breaks away.* CHLOE *stares after him.*)

Daphne. Daphne!

CHLOE: (*Smiles, happy, suddenly realizing*) Oh, Daphne?

(LIONEL, *breaking away from the congratulations of the buyers, comes over to* CHLOE.)

LIONEL: (*Melancholic*) Chloe . . .

(*They start to dance.*)

Is that all there is? All that work and this is it?

CHLOE: Well, it's always more fun to get ready than to arrive.

(JOHN *regards his son proudly.* LIONEL *and* CHLOE *dance out of shot.* STEWART *and* DAPHNE *watch them go past.*)

86

DAPHNE: Too bad Lionel's gay.

> (CHLOE *and* LIONEL *dance back into shot.*)

LIONEL: Chloe, I'm not gay.

CHLOE: I know, you're miserable.

LIONEL: No, I mean I'm not that way.

CHLOE: What way are you, then?

LIONEL: I'm a closet heterosexual. I was afraid no one would take me seriously in the fashion world if I was straight. The fact is, I'm crazy about you.

> (*They sweep past* JOHN, *who hears this and punches the air joyously.*)

CHLOE: (*Surprised*) Oh God, Lionel? I'll have to adjust to that . . . I think I'm going to like it.

> (THE SHIT *and* JEAN *whirl past* STEWART.)

JEAN: Will you have me?

THE SHIT: Of course I will.

JEAN: Are you sure?

THE SHIT: Sure I'm sure.

JEAN: I'm so happy.

> (STEWART *bristles. He strains to hear more, but they move out of earshot.*)

THE SHIT: We'll have to work at it. Four or five hours a day, doing the moves, and when we're not dancing, you'll be sewing sequins.

JEAN: We'll win every over-forty-fives in the land.

> (*They swirl out of shot.*
>
> STEWART *is stung.*)

STEWART: (*To* DAPHNE) Your mother's a beautiful woman.

> (TOM *comes up and grabs* DAPHNE *into his arms, swirling her off into the trees.*)

TOM: I love you.

DAPHNE: Are you sure you're not making a mistake?

TOM: I've made a lot of those, but this is not one of them.

> (*They kiss.*
>
> STEWART *sets off with a determined stride. He lurches towards* SHERYL. *She shrinks back.*)

STEWART: I better grab a chair before the music stops.

SHERYL: You should get help, Mr McBain. I know a very good homoeopathic psychotherapist.

(STEWART *is not looking at her but past her, at* JEAN *and* THE SHIT. SHERYL *is left talking to the air again.*

As STEWART *lurches across the dance floor,* MARCUS *passes him, approaching* SHERYL.)

MARCUS: How could I win your heart?

SHERYL: Easy. Just promise not to walk off when I'm in the middle of a sentence.

(STEWART *steps up behind* THE SHIT *and taps him briskly on the shoulder.*)

STEWART: (*Through his teeth*) Do you mind?

THE SHIT: Just keeping her warm for you.

(THE SHIT *graciously gives way to* STEWART *with a bow.* STEWART *acknowledges him with a nod and a smile.* STEWART *takes his wife in his arms and dances with her stiffly, counting softly under his breath to keep in step.*)

STEWART: One, two, three and one, two, three.

JEAN: Darling, don't do it by numbers, do it from the heart.

STEWART: I'll do the best I can, Jean.

(*It is an apology.*)

JEAN: (*Contentedly*) Well, nobody can do better than that.

(*Their dancing becomes better and better, and soon* STEWART *stops counting.*

The end titles come up over a succession of Chloe's calendar paintings, finishing with Déjeuner sur l'Herbe.)

Faber Film

Woody Allen
Alan Bennett
John Boorman
Sergei Eisenstein
Peter Greenaway
Graham Greene
John Grierson
Trevor Griffiths
Christopher Hampton
David Hare
Derek Jarman
Neil Jordan
Hanif Kureishi
Akira Kurosawa
Louis Malle
Harold Pinter
Dennis Potter
Satyajit Ray
Martin Scorsese
Andrey Tarkovsky
Robert Towne
François Truffaut
Andrzej Wajda
Wim Wenders